O.O.O.

✦

Obsessing On Obsession
(The Documentary)

Mitch Reed

iUniverse, Inc.
New York   Bloomington

O.O.O.

Obsessing On Obsession (The Documentary)

iUniverse books may be ordered through booksellers or by contacting:

iUniverse
1663 Liberty Drive
Bloomington, IN 47403
www.iuniverse.com
1-800-Authors (1-800-288-4677)

ISBN: 978-0-595-53219-3 (pbk)
ISBN: 978-0-595-63280-0 (ebk)

Printed in the United States of America

iUniverse rev. date: 11/19/08

"Hamas official Mushir Masri, in a fiery speech Friday to thousands of Hamas supporters in Gaza, said the meetings with Carter were proof that Hamas was not a terrorist group, but a national liberation movement."—*Fox News.com website, reported 4/18/08*

What a crock of...crap.

Preface

Before I begin, I would like to share with all of you reading this narrative that I have intentionally tried to lighten the weight of this material up, so that its impact is softened and more palpable. I realize that some of what you will read in this book will shock many of you, although I hope it will not offend you.

My first confession is that I consider myself a compassionate conservative, and I clearly believe that all the assorted parties have made mistakes and errors…all of them! Yes, I beat up the left at times, but I do likewise with the President too, and find myself more than once supporting the left's lofty environmental goals.

While I hope to raise your curiosity enough to watch *Obsession* for yourselves, it is not my wish to frighten you with the material contained within my book. So wherever possible, and as professionally as possible, I have added humor or at least sarcasm, to lighten the impact of this book's weighty subject matter. Accordingly, if any of my comments or language offends you, please accept my sincere apology now.

Mitch Reed

We live in a dangerous world today. Apparently our humanity on this long-suffering mid-size planet of yours and mine has ebbed into a new all-time-low level of morality and depravity. So much so, that a radical, religious ideology now seeks our immediate destruction to free the world of our outlandish modernity and freedoms.

Yes—we are that horrible rogue nation that chose to give the world...Lucy and Ricky, Gilligan and the Skipper, and of course...the Brady Bunch, as our own unique version of spreading the gospel of tolerance, peace, and freedom—instead of giving ourselves blindly to the Koran and Allah.

Candidly, we may soon be in desperate times; so it is therefore my goal to reach you somehow, and warn you through my pen, as the old adage goes. As a concerned American 'infidel' you see, you might say I'm anxious to do so—as there is solace in numbers. To that end, the first section of this book is meant as a complimentary prerequisite to sitting down yourself like I did one quiet evening, and beginning your education in religious-based terrorism by watching a singular documentary—a very powerful film indeed. This then, is the focus of Part One of this book.

Simply said, make sure you are watching this film wearing brown slacks—for your own protection of embarrassing yourself as this film may scare the sh_t—right out of you.

Honestly, I had heard a little about the film Obsession in the months prior to purchasing it, in the form of trailers and commentary on cable television, talk radio, and such. That being said, I had no idea then, how deeply and profoundly it would affect me. Perhaps others were less impacted than me, but that's also understandable.

Both my undergraduate and postgraduate studies you see were focused on the behavioral sciences. This includes majoring in Political Science as an undergraduate, followed by postgraduate studies including a residency program as a

Subconscious Behaviorist, focusing on human suggestible behavior. Those studies included becoming a trained clinical hypnotist in 1969, and later choosing to study further. I became a Master Hypnotist, and followed that by further studying in a clinical residency setting, culminating in becoming a Certified Clinical Hypnotherapist in 1990.

As a behaviorist alone, I know the power of propaganda and repetitive suggestion all too well...and the consequences of same on a blindsided mind. I am well read and schooled on various techniques in brainwashing, sensory depravation, and suggestive influences in general—I therefore, could not let any of this go. It has nagged on me daily since first watching the documentary.

If I could have my druthers right now, I would not be writing this book at this moment altogether. I would be instead, continuing the promotion for my current book, a fictional novel, entitled—Blessings of the Father—Book One published by iUniverse, that will grow to a saga in six volumes. It is a mainstream novel, lighthearted, and a cheerful work of fiction that in Book One effectively weaves a serious theme painlessly into a larger story. You see, it eases us all through the fear of death and dying, by anecdotally sharing actual scientific and Para-psychological empirical evidence. It's all from my perspective as a Hypnotherapist and regressing more than four hundred (400) people back to over one thousand (1000) past lives over a thirty four year history. I fell into my first past-life encounter inadvertently with a client in 1974. I then spent the subsequent two years remaining pragmatic and more skeptical than believer myself, until overwhelming evidence for the phenomenon convinced me and I reached a personal enlightenment! Foremost within the evidence was the pioneering work of the brilliant researcher and Doctor, Raymond Moody. The conclusion becomes self-evident and simple—the fear of death that our western society seems to suffer at the hands of, is something everyone can benefit from overcoming and can be easily accomplished by opening one's mind to the various points of evidence. That became my goal for Book One of this saga; Blessings of the Father.

Yet sometimes in life, something vital or enormous steps in and motivates you to change course, and so it was with me and this new book...Obsessing On Obsession that I felt compelled to write. Let me offer you an opening glimpse into this conflict by way of example:

Does it trouble you as much as I, that **on a daily basis,** somewhere in the Middle East, countless radical Imams or Clerics repetitively call for the destruction of the United States and the West, to their loyal and fundamentalist congregations? If it does, then you understand my urgency.

The warning signs are all there folks, so much so, that the message and the raw intensity of this documentary's power has compelled me literally to where we are today. While you read this preface, I—Mr. Macho, continue to shake somewhat in my boots just thinking about the enormity of it.

You might be asking yourselves; "If Islamic Fanaticism has become so mainstream, widespread, and serious—why haven't I seen anything reported before now? You know, I watch TV, I read my daily newspaper,—it can't be so serious if I see and read nothing about it...can it?"

In as many words...yes it is friends!

And you know, perhaps the greatest irony of this whole sorted and sad affair, is that the one specific group of professionals that we should all be able to count on and to thank for exposing this global threat—has remained...all but silent! But worse than that, **our media** has turned a deft and audacious ear to the signs of danger all around us, ignoring and minimizing it, even in the face of a direct threat to all of us...but why?

Why indeed. There certainly cannot be a reasonable explanation for their lack of interest in this threat, other than the obvious...that being their political bias and persuasion.

Naturally, I feel strongly that media bias is in play here, with minimal attention being paid as the result. The few stories now finally being reported have only become a more recent phenomenon with the surge's success, and are never given urgent attention.

Perhaps secondarily to this bias, is the media's sad allegiance to political correctness. And it is clear that political correctness on many fronts, may well lead to our downfall in the fight ahead—but at least some Americans will likely be happy with our newly acquired skills in sensitivity! As Obsession so powerfully demonstrates: *"We are being strangled by our own Political Correctness!"*

Let me spell it out for you America—radical Islam has declared war on the West! This is not an exaggeration, overstatement, or dramatic fluff…this is fact! Part One of this book will illustrate how these radical crusaders place the highest value on their own honorable death (what they call Shahid) while they attempt to kill all of their enemies of Islam at the same time…us!

Forgive me but these nut jobs feel as strongly about their own honorable death, as we in the West (are diametrically opposed) and would naturally place the highest value on human life itself! This very truth is frightening to the core when you consider the ramifications of it.

To think that any reasonably intelligent person could actually believe that there is a greater value in death by martyring oneself, over the sanctity of life itself, seems unfathomable within our Western culture, yet within their radical Islamic culture, honestly the opposite rings true. From a perspective of warfare, having to do battle with these kooks—knowing they welcome death right along with killing you, is perhaps the most frightening aspect of this to contend with.

And few will be spared by these extremists. All non-Muslims and moderate Muslims fall into the category of Islam's enemies too, especially those in the West!

There is another perhaps more dangerous element to this cultural conflict with radical Islam. The onslaught of this fanatical element is multifaceted in its efforts and fronts, and it's difficult to expose it true motives at times as they follow a sort of religious deception. Part Two of this book is acutely focused on this aspect of the problem.

These terrorists are masters at deception and lying about their motives, and make no mistake—to them, this is one global war against us, and to begin with—it's a transnational war!

We are not able to label these players as simply terrorist states or the Axis of Terror as Mr. Bush once chose to characterize them. No, in reality, this is a war essentially of individual players, being backed by State sponsors, so President Bush was only partially right...oh forgive me—I meant to say...correct!

The documentary exposes the breadth of the Holy Jihad against us in historical context in Part One, and through my impressions of what I took away from the film.

In Part Two with Obsession as my inspiration, I dug up dirt...lots of it, on what's really going on in this conflict and where it might all lead. So I put forward some of the potential consequences, and expose some of the possible strategies of their playbook, such as our current energy crisis and their possible plans for Israel.

Do you realize that particularly in Europe, we are seeing that as often as not, these extremists are now native-born citizens, fighting Jihad for their god Allah...Part Two explains why? Irrespective of their own government—their loyalty seems to lie with Allah...and let their native country be damned...for they feel no nationalistic loyalty!

I feel the documentary in Part One clearly makes the case that the biggest mistake we in the West make about this enemy is in failing to see the obvious—from the enemy's perspective, that this war is certainly global, and it is a single threat! We in the West stupidly see this as separate terror 'incidents'...

A WTC tower here, a London bomber there. We need to wake up and smell the C-4 explosive—think of this conflict as a pandemic of pure evil that is intent on destruction like a virus the world over! In Part Two, I illustrate the creative ways these combatants hope to defeat us…one way or the other. And if they can't do it militarily, they'll certainly settle for financially.

You will likely come to understand early on in this book, what's so frightening about Obsession the movie—is its honest candor. It eloquently puts forward this well-researched and accepted argument: We are not in a simple political war of terror. No…we are truly in a Holy War for our very survival. As only one example, is the side-by-side comparisons and nexus the producers have drawn from the fascists of Nazi Germany, and they demonstrate poignantly as such, that this threat is anything but new!

And in the case of this analysis, it is my opinion Ladies and Gentlemen that we are dealing in simplest terms with a perverse ideology. One that has been, and continues to be…infiltrated and absorbed into as many Islamic minds as possible through their mosques, madrassas, and the like. We learn later, how this is being done with our own oil money… currently to the tune of $14 billion *being put directly into the hands of the very enemy who is trying to destroy us!*

Like Hitler and the Nazis that these Islamic leaders have so closely modeled themselves, they have become quite effective in infiltrating diverse populations around the globe.

Clearly they are engaging in creating separatist communities within an excess of fifty countries right now! And in those countries, they are inspiring modest civil disobedience and unrest—strictly for now. What happens tomorrow, only time will tell? Meanwhile, they answer only…to their radical Imams, Clerics, and of course—Allah.

The next logical step of these separatist communities is naturally to serve as home base within those countries for when the next phase of this Holy War escalates…and Part Two shows you who to thank for all of this radical ideology.

Impossible you say…ludicrous you contend? Alright have it your way, but consider these facts before you say it isn't so:

Proof of these separatist communities and their destructive power can be seen in the fact that all of the London bombers of July 2005 were all homegrown British-born and raised, not unlike many of the French rioters that caused all of that trouble more recently in Paris, according to Obsession.

And yes, before you ask, we ourselves are now being infiltrated and getting closer to being invaded by this ideological virus. Rather than a state-sponsored army, we'll first see simple issues and mild protests. You see, when we read in the paper that Muslim taxi drivers in Kansas City are **demanding** foot baths be installed inside their airport bathrooms, and we don't question…the why of it, we edge a little closer to our enemy's goal. You see, their request is not merely political correctness—that's only the justification. And it's used against us and to my way of thinking—it portends what a mature version of this local Radical Islamic community will represent. So we fall a little deeper into their deception and closer to their goal of destroying us from within—believe me. And we will have political correctness to thank for that… and our enemy knows this and abducts it to its cause, and not to our intended common good!

If I'm correct, look for Kansas City to become a hot spot for attracting many more radical Muslim residents in the future, and for that city to have increasing unrest perhaps on various issues and levels, sooner than other US cities.

So see, when and if we are conquered, it won't come strictly from a bomb, medical malady or a biological cause. This one is much worse…we will succumb to infiltration and the loss of our American way of life **from within**!

I can't over-emphasize this enough…I pray that you get your hands on this documentary. Buy it, rent it…or borrow it…then watch it.

Please don't view it alone! Watch it with your spouses or significant others or friends, and then with your responsible, mature teens and adult children. Under no circumstances should you expose this film to your innocent children.

For the record, I am not in any way or fashion affiliated with the producers of Obsession. I have no vested or otherwise financial relationship or interest with this film or these producers. As a matter of fact and record, I have purposely not had contact with the producers in any way, once the movie was shipped to my address as a direct purchaser. In other words, this narrative is a completely liberated effort on my part, to give you my wholly independent impressions of the movie's power and message. In the latter half of the book I offer my predictions, their consequences and strategies and playbooks. In the final analysis then, I am clearly...

OBSESSING ON OBSESSION...THE DOCUMENTARY.

A quick word about citations. In Part One, I am almost exclusively offering my impressions based on the material from Obsession the movie. Therefore, I will only reference the source of outside or independent sources and cite them where appropriate. All other quotations can be considered to stem from the movie Obsession, and its many expert speakers, so the reference is considered made by the 'absence' of a citation itself. In the second section of the book...I'm mostly putting forward, my own opinions and thoughts, so citations there are limited to generally outside quotes that support my comments or contentions.

Now read, remember, and react!

Mitch Reed

Contents

PART ONE

Impressions of a Powerful
Documentary.

First Impression

Chapter One

Be Afraid…Yes Very Afraid

I want you to keep an open mind to what I'm going to contend in the following paragraphs. What follows is not an effort to alarm you casually with questionable or refutable facts…not at all. What you are about to read is real, it is happening now…and it affects the future of both you and your entire family. So it is my simple goal to persuade you to put aside seventy minutes and devote an evening to watching this film, for: *"The tentacles of terrorism are reaching out to every corner of the world."*

Welcome to: Radical Islamic Fundamentalism, and simply stated they'd like you dead—now deal with that! Why not think on it a bit, and then ask yourself if that reality sits well with you, like singing three verses of 'Kumbaya' around a campfire?

Have you done everything you've dreamed of before moving on to the next life, or are you still trying to accomplish something more for yourself or your family? Have you made enough money in this life? Have you acquired the most toys yet, and is your house so large it has its own zip code? Did you remember to order that hot new flat screen…and can you even reach your shrink with this latest crisis you're reading about—right now?

As pathetic as the above commentary may seem and what it says about our collective vanity and materiality—it is also the sad truth of what these radicals would truly like to accomplish for themselves. These zealots strive for the annihilation of all Western culture and modernity. Their theological leaders have empowered each of their approximate two hundred (200) million followers to serve as Allah's divine executioners! ***"And they're going to kill you because the nice little preacher in the Mosque told them too!"*** Is that okay with you? Go on and ask yourself.

I'm now going to reintroduce you to a two-word statement of fact that applies here…and sadly I'm not speaking of Hollywood's latest fictional epic film either. It's:

-HOLY WAR-

There I've said it, and these radicals behind this modern chapter of Holy War, simply want you in a body bag with a toe tag. And believe me—there may be many!

Don't believe me…then watch Obsession repeatedly. And please do not be so naïve as to confuse this global conflict with a simple political dispute, this is beyond that. While admittedly an unpopular claim, I'm talking about something on a par with a clash of civilizations here.

When we talk about a modern Holy War, many among us might wonder what that entails definitively and it's a fair question. In the past, a Holy War was any war that had as its focus some dispute based upon religious principle, issues, aggression, expansion of religious dogma, or any attempt to defend a religious belief…that was then.

I believe this modern Holy War, is somewhat more akin to a contemporary video game of sorts. It offers this commentary: If you don't agree with us, believe as we do, if we do not like you, and if you and your country represent anything 'modern'...we will slit your throat, spill your blood, and earn a free game bonus in heaven for our efforts... especially if we die!

And here again, no disrespect to President Bush...oh what the hell—let's have at least a little disrespect—but the two interchangeable terms de jour at his White House— Terror War and War on Terror, don't even come close to what we're dealing with here! For one thing, the absence of any mention of the religious contingent in these terms implies a more secular, political issue...when it certainly is not.

This war has everything to do with religion, so repeat after me...this is a Holy War—case closed, pure and simple.

Mr. President, your time at the reins is nearly through— eight challenging years. Yet before the upcoming election is decided, and you ride off into the sunset towards Crawford, your fellow countrymen need to hear you admit that we are truly fighting a Holy War, and not simply a secular, political war on terror.

So come clean Mr. President, and affirm my faith in your humanity and candor. You have consistently put your concerns and beliefs for our country's welfare, way ahead of your own popularity and positive opinion polls. Let me suggest that you finish the job and tell us—all of it, within reason of course. You don't have to frighten us—but you need to empower us. Don't mince words—just give us the bottom line. Someone has to unite us once more Mr. President and you succeeded before, why not do it again? Let's send a message to the next Congress and to our enemies as well...that we are now wise to those who would do us evil, and we understand what we must do to prevail.

But when I say 'these radical players' allow me to clarify who these players are, and more importantly who they—most certainly are not. As expected, they are not your typical law-abiding, tolerant, and peace-loving Muslim. These peaceful persons make up an estimated +/- 85% of the world's 1.2 billion Muslims...and they...and the Muslim faith they represent, are being threatened and held hostage too by these fanatics, perhaps as vehemently as us.

My heart goes out to these people. Like us, they are the intended victims of this global conflict. You see, the fanatical Muslims I am speaking of—are the fundamental Radical Islamics...these radical fanatics—want the non-believing Muslim destroyed too, as much as any Jew, Christian or other Westerner. They call all of us swine, infidels, or Kuffars which literally translates to 'non-believer'.

Candidly though, I must reference Obsession again as I am likewise concerned about the abundant silence coming from within the moderate Muslim communities. It is important honestly, that we know that the silence within this worldwide community is based on fear, and not—sympathy under the mere veneer of peacefulness. Somehow, we need to hear more from this silent majority, if not with words, then with deeds—and then we must support their efforts as pronounced as possible.

The fundamental Islamic fanatics refer to their conflict against us as Jihad or Holy War. According to the film, the literal translation for Jihad is: 'To struggle within oneself' or 'my struggle'. And the film points out, poignantly in fact that the definition of Hitler's Mein Kampf was: 'My struggle'.

So let's see if we have the facts straight. One, these fanatics are already fighting a Holy War...and not a political one. Two, this Jihad is against the West and life itself. Three, everyone in the West is to be conquered or eliminated. Therefore all Western nations and every Jew, Christian, Kuffar Muslim,

Buddhist, and Hindu is at risk! Yes its true, they don't like any of these peaceful Eastern religions either!

Now what do you suggest we all do about this? Believe me; many people in our country have very strong and passionate opinions on the subject of the greater Middle East, so let's look at a few of them.

To begin with, we could listen to our liberal friends for instance, and 'redeploy' from this unlawful war we can't win in Iraq anyway? Forget the fact that **Osama Bin Laden himself has declared the Iraqi War the central front in this Jihad against the West.**

Or let's believe as Mr. Obama does that countries such as Iran, Syria, and No. Korea, Venezuela, and other rogue nations pose nothing as dangerous as former foes such as the Soviet Union because they're small, insignificant countries with minuscule military budgets. More than likely, this is that fantastic Obama 'judgment' we've all heard so much about, that must be it, right? Yet let me ask you something Senator:

You know Barry—oh forgive me, Senator Obama, back in 1941, it took nearly half the Japanese fleet and most of their air force to attack us in your beloved Hawaii at Pearl Harbor and kill twenty six hundred (2600) Americans on one quiet Sunday Morning. Yet how 'big' of a military did it take to attack us on 9/11, some sixty years later, when we saw 3000 innocent Americans murdered in the short expanse of a few hours time? **It took nineteen (count them 19) fanatical zealots...with box cutters for an arsenal!** And Senator, how many individual Jihadists would it take to carry one dirty bomb undetected inside an innocuous suitcase, into New York City's JFK airport and detonate it, while five hundred more of this ilk, without warning, does the same exact thing in five hundred other American airports and public transportation hubs...**simultaneously**?

You see Senator, this is transnational warfare made up of small groups of individual Jihad terrorists, or cells—think of them as a computer worm infiltrating and inching its way along and destroying your hard drive in the process. There are big players too—the state players, but they seem to prefer so far, to play only by proxy, but they include some of these rouge countries who you would meet without any conditions. Let's look at Iran in Iraq shall we? They are funding, training, and supplying the insurgents aligned with al-Qaida, while Syria and Iran influence Lebanon, supporting their wholly owned organization of mirth and merriment…Hezbollah! And all the while, Jimmy Carter's favorite guests for tea and cookies…Hamas, are benefiting greatly from Iran and Syria's support too.

This Holy War Senator presents us with highly unique circumstances and a differently motivated warrior as our enemy, and an entirely new dynamic in those players' intentions. Perhaps as a freshman Senator without direct experience in Foreign Policy or as a Commander-In-Chief, you might wish to reconsider your position?

Then again, Senator, Obama's judgment is purported to be wise and astute, so perhaps he knows better. Yet then again, he's the very first Presidential Candidate I can recall during a time of war, to actually tell you what he's going to do policy-wise with that war as president…before he even goes over and meets with the generals and leaders in the theatre to discuss it…what a great mentalist this man must be!

And I have another question for America's newest foreign policy expert Senator: Your contention is that you got it right on Iraq. Might I inquire as to who told you something so premature? Sorry senator, but most students of history would tell you that a proclamation of this sort is certainly impulsive on your part, and then some!

Like every other major event or war in our country's two hundred and thirty plus year history, insight along with full disclosure of the facts only comes with the eventual outcome of the war and the passage of time. Often, it takes a lot of time depending upon the complexities, security, and sensitivity issues! So let's be honest Senator, what you offered was little more than political rhetoric and postulating and nothing more.

Senator, with the Iraq war not over, and still being fought aggressively, with ultimate success or failure (and the consequences of same) to be evaluated, analyzed, and debated, you're a bit hasty.

To be fair, if you want to purport that it has been a long, painful, and protracted war—fine…I'll concede that point. It's also fair to contend as I do, that there are mixed results so far to show for our sacrifice of over four thousand (4000) American dead, and so we have a right to question, like you do, if this conflict was worth that horrible sacrifice at times. And with many in our country unhappy and frustrated and fed up with this conflict, that's also understandable yet all of this is still missing the point and therefore…wrong!

Yet let me remind you Senator that you are claiming in my opinion, an erroneous and dangerous premature victory on your judgment Senator…and it may come back to haunt you! Current conditions in Iraq tell a far different story and picture than you portray. Here's a little example of what I mean:

One of your accomplishments since being elected into the Senate was your appointment onto the all-important and powerful Senate Foreign Relations Committee. No doubt earned by your breathtaking speech at the last Democratic Convention…damn you're so good at reading from those side-to-side teleprompters, you're as hypnotic to watch as a pair of windshield wipers! Isn't it strange though, that the minute they ask you something off the prompter…you babble like a three-year-old in toilet training!

But hey, everyone worth their salt knows that you have been seen from the very beginning as an 'up and comer' within the party ranks, so your appointment might well have been expected on this basis alone. Lastly, anyone who can defeat the Clinton machine is certainly no chump.

At any rate, what I find so personally interesting about that famous Obama 'judgment' is how questionable it can be at times. In short sir, you have yet to provide any kind of track record to be touting to the American public or anyone else for that matter, let's just call it like it is. Candidly you excel at many things, and perhaps after a dozen more years of public service, you'll be ready for the ultimate position. For right now though, I would lean you towards limiting your tryouts to Dancing with the Stars. I have to say, I caught you on Ellen too and you do bust a move—so presidential. And did I hear you proclaim—"merci beaucoup" to Ellen for providing you the opportunity?

Listen Senator, don't beat yourself up. But since we still seem to be on the subject, I do have one final illustration to put to you. Not only did you personally vote against the Surge, but you sought out an alternative of complete withdrawal of our troops in Iraq by this past March of 2008 I believe! So were you right about the Surge, Senator? Was that wonderful judgment of yours—correct? And how about what you yourself, suggested in its stead—total withdrawal, was that such good 'judgment'?

By most standards and even the ever-reliable bias of the main street press—the Surge has not only turned the tide it has succeeded overall. Yet how would that have happened if the country had followed '*your*' judgment' and we had already withdrawn all of our troops instead, last March…was it? Do you think that Al Qaida in Iraq would have been on the ropes as they are today—following your 'judgment' call?

I am reminded that today, because of the Surge's success, American fatalities in Iraq are at their lowest levels in years. This last May we lost 19 American Military heroes, and while that is 19 too many as we all know, I would point out that that is fewer than the number of citizens innocently killed within

Senator Obama's own beloved city of Chicago in the same period in violent crime alone!

You know Senator, Chicago murders alone topped 5,000 in 2005 while you were still there…do you think that anyone in Chicago ever wonders whether it's worth the risk to live there? After all, they had 25% more deaths by murder, than Iraq has had in American casualties…and in one fifth of the time! Isn't it just possible that some risks are worth taking and some battles worth fighting?

As realists, we need to talk straight here. I know we could bury our heads in the sand, and just pretend we are not in the fight of our collective lives. Sadly this may be what the good Senator's flawed judgment is telling him to do, and that's fine for him as long as he's not elected President.

But how do smart, knowledgeable Americans, ignore and put aside the knowledge that *one* dirty bomb is capable of murdering *ten thousand* or so innocent victims!—So how does five hundred of these bombs stack up? *The potential mass murder of five million Americans in ten seconds time*…that's how, vs. the mere five hundred suicide-bomber casualties on their side! Remember, it took nineteen of these bastards to murder three thousand (3,000) of us…*Now—Do I have your attention?*

Moving right along down our list of outspoken Americans, here's one of my favorites. Perhaps we should continue to celebrate our denial and flaunt it in the face of the facts—like the Michael Moore's of this world have done. When Moore states in a press conference that "there is no terrorist threat" I honestly cringe" Unlike his orchestrated documentary Fahrenheit 911, which more accurately could allude perhaps—to his weight, than to the tragedy that took place on that date, Obsession is real and he would gain much to watch it himself.

As I sit here and listen to the campaign rhetoric of 2008 and specifically the calls for withdrawal from the war in Iraq,

I have to ask myself—why is it so hard to understand these sentiments? As a society, we Americans detest war after all. By nature we are not a warring people, we're generally pacifists by and large. Hell, we'd rather shop or jog to the gym in other words. We have proven time and again that we love peace and typically deplore war.

And we are a compassionate people. Just this year alone, our gifts to charities and efforts the world over, totaled over three hundred (300) billion dollars! Do you realize that's the equivalent of over $1,000 donated for every man, woman, and unemployed child in this country! Christ…that's unheard of and it demonstrates my point: We've always shown compassion, through our financial support for more impoverished and challenged nations, than any other nation on earth, while consistently demonstrating that we are not Imperialists. When called upon, we have helped to liberate millions of innocent people, and writing the first check at the time of some natural disaster half way around the globe.

And yes, as a superpower, we have been less than perfect, we've made some stupid mistakes. Often when we have been forced to choose sides, it was strictly for short-term political expediency. Rarely are we offered the luxury of making a choice with sufficient knowledge to know the true friend from enemy anyway, so we typically hedge our debts as best we can, and suffer through the mistakes made…years later. Of course it's easy playing Monday morning quarterback anyway—isn't it? Here's a perfect poignant example. We initially supported Bin Laden's forces when they were conveniently fighting the Soviets for us by proxy in Afghanistan. Now we know enough to see the error of our ways, don't we? And no one's exempt from these quick decisions either, more recently, President Clinton logically backed Iran's involvement in Bosnia.

Yet there are those among us that believe that because of these isolated shortsighted mistakes, our country is to blame for every single problem we face in foreign policy, rather than open their minds to the obvious dynamic of incalculable consequences. This is so unfair on its face—and it is certainly a flawed conclusion to draw upon, in my opinion. No country plays chess perfectly besides which, do they?

After a protracted conflict such as this, it's natural that we don't want to fight the war on the Iraqi front indefinitely, and we won't. But I also know that we must not leave Iraq or any front in this Holy War without winning first!

Yes, let's get this out of the way right now, all right? I just equated the Iraqi war as a front in this Holy War...and why wouldn't I? Let's not forget:

Given what I've already said about what's happening in the Arab world, could there be any doubt that Iraq is surely the main front at this moment in time...Bin Laden's past statements seem to confirm this.

Historically speaking, the Middle East has been a hotbed of problems for decades. You know, many people if asked, would say that this entire Jihad' against us began on September 11th, 2001, but they would be sadly mistaken...by more than twenty years!

From my perspective as a behaviorist, I agree with what has been put forward by the producers of Obsession...these fanatical roots go back much further. The violence against us itself—began in 1979, yet the ideology itself, dates back much further, in fact to the late 1930's! So today's violence is nothing new, but the tactics and the dynamics of the enemy have definitely changed.

And to be fair, we adjusted to the threat militarily pretty well. We likely trumped these Islamic radicals by attacking Saddam Hussein when we did; and according to Matthew Continetti in the Weekly Standard in their 6/09/08 issue: ***"The president denied the Jihadists an ally by removing Saddam Hussein from power in Iraq."—Matthew Continetti June 9, 2008.***

Of course beyond Mr. Continetti's quote, we are not going to be able to validate his contention without the hindsight of history in perhaps another twenty years or so.

Even though our involvement in this Jihad effectively began with Afghanistan as our enemy, this was never the only front in this greater war—at least from the Jihadists' perspective. For them, they are fighting for Allah—the world over!

So this is a single global conflict as the film points out! And these fanatics have not sat idly by outside of the Middle East either…have they? Before and since the attacks of 9/11, we have seen major attacks and incidents worldwide, haven't we? Madrid, Bali, London, Russia, and even in Saudi Arabia which is telling—to name merely a sampling.

Ironically it's a little funny, but crappy intelligence might just save our collective asses after all! When future historians look back at our entry into this conflict and the Iraq decision specifically from the administration's perspective, inaccurate intelligence will likely be at the forefront in their analysis and final opinion. It was carried over from so many varied sources, in addition to several past administrations, that it seemed to take on a life of its own, if judged now by its inaccuracy. And it fundamentally played therefore, into the current administration's focus on possible offensive solutions following our initial routing of the Taliban in Afghanistan.

Only years from now will we be able to clearly judge if this may have well led us to a poorly planned phase two of the war with Iraq, or maybe not? The Surge offensive may yet prove that our phase two mistakes weren't insurmountable. Under the best of circumstances, it is hoped that our entry into the Iraqi conflict, will prove pivotal to our ultimate global success against this enemy one day…I pray it should only be so.

In summation then, its way too premature to put any label on the Iraq war, either failure or success. We know we've made tactical errors, yet we also recognize that the terrorists for one, never believed we would ever rise united to combat them, in either Afghanistan or Iraq. Their leaders told their followers that we were weak and unwilling to fight...and that taking down our financial icons alone would likely destroy us. Well—they were wrong friend...dead wrong.

And hell, I know we want it over, I know we'd like our guys and gals, sons and daughters, brothers and sisters home, but can we afford to stop the momentum now? No we mustn't...we dare not.

If you are of the mind that leaving Iraq now will end this worldwide conflict and peace will ensue instead...dream on! Simply handing these fanatical zealots a victory now, by premature retreat, would send the worst possible message at a critical juncture (a change in US administrations). And it would send the message to these warped crusaders **to carry on** and that not only are we weak, but ready to be conquered, dominated, and slaughtered...all in the name of Allah.

And think back to those mass graves that have been uncovered in Iraq, and the torture chambers revealed too. These certainly don't send a message of free lives under Saddam's regime either, so at least we're fighting for something honorable in Iraq. More importantly, who would the Iraqi people prefer to have influencing their country...Saddam or their new democratically elected Parliament?

And yet, this is all real, it's happening today...and it's not your fathers' kind of warfare either! Your father's enemies wanted to live...what nerve they had! And more often then not, they came from some particular country we happened to be at war with.

Honestly, from a war strategist's point-of-view...what do you do with a warrior that has no particular motivation to physically survive the conflict? One who would gladly sacrifice themselves...along with you—to Jihad's glory for Allah, and those 72 waiting virgins in heaven, rather than saving their own hide? So they fight for Allah exclusively, and not out of loyalty for any particular country, as I've mentioned.

We simply cannot abandon this fight now, were in it, so I suggest that we all just swallow our pride and grow the hell up!

Not to go off on a tangent, but it's a telling statement to me however, that the Jihadists' own fanatical leaders, do not seem to share that same zeal and enthusiasm to join Allah's embrace so soon…and meet those 72 young virgins—what a shock that is…and a pity. One thing is clear; we have never had an enemy dynamic like this.

You know on that subject, like many, I have often wondered and conjectured if the White House was really so off base about this whole war on terror stuff in the first place? It's likely that this administration knows we're fighting a more serious religious conflict, and far beyond a mere warped political ideology.

I speculate that from the beginning, well before we entered Afghanistan that President Bush did not feel he could sell a Holy War politically—out of the box. How could he hope for support from the Arab Street, let alone our own people and allies…even after 9/11? I mean, think about it:

Let's say this president had gone on the tube after 9/11 and said we were in a Holy War of Armageddon proportions? A true clash of civilizations, with an enemy that saw the conflict as a fight to the death at all costs, and all in the name of their God. Christ—we would have had the poor bastard committed, let's be honest! Sadly though, it appears now that all of that commentary would have proven closely accurate!

If you think back on some of the White House's earliest comments on this new enemy, they really didn't mince words on the severity of the threat as I recall though, did they? And while they glossed over the religious aspects…they never denied a radical Islamic ideology existed, either.

And then came those other troubling little signs sporadically popping up on the news and internet after we liberated the country initially: Suicide bombers; men, women and sometimes-even children…blowing themselves apart along with other…infidels—all for Allah. Kidnappings and abductions ending in televised beheadings for the entire (Western) world to witness on the internet…and fear. And the intended targets were often innocent civilians. They included journalists, non-Muslim clergy (naturally), and regular civilians…all major threats to this enemy apparently. Yes, they're a tolerant lot, aren't they?

I remember too, a young couple, caught kissing in public, and so they were put on trail for their heinous crime against Allah. After being found guilty, the two young lovers were given the equivalent of getting slapped on the wrist by Allah—**they were stoned to death** as just and fair punishment!

Countless young women have been killed by their brothers and/or fathers for bringing disgrace to their families for daring to marry a man for love? It happened again this week…but with a twist. This time, it was a Pakistani Muslim father living outside Atlanta Georgia! Yes, here in America, and he killed his own daughter for wanting to divorce her husband from an arranged marriage that took place in Pakistan.

And I understand that only this week, Iran has approved formal sentencing for eight Iranian women accused of Adultery, they too will be stoned to death. In all seriousness, let's pray for these innocent women.

Happily though, there have been other signs too. Signs we can take heart in. Like purple thumbs held proudly in the air as twelve million Iraqis went to vote in free elections. Children smiling and playing in the streets and markets reopening. A working parliamentary government, a fledging democracy taking control of its destiny and reconciling old animosities and finding democratic solutions to old problems, while more elections are planned for January of 09.

Most recently, they have begun sharing the country's wealth among the three regions of the country which was a critical milestone. Fifteen of the eighteen milestones have been met already that Congress demanded. Frankly, I'd like to see our 110th Congress that efficacious themselves for a change!

And ask yourself this: Under all of these circumstances, what will deploying from Iraq accomplish, or might it put things at further risk instead? Do you remember the millions slaughtered in Southeast Asia following our deployment from Vietnam? And back then, we just called our deployment there—what it was…defeat! Take Cambodia alone, subsequent to the end of the Vietnam conflict, over two million died in Pol Pot's genocide and killing fields, do we want to risk something similar in Iraq?

Our dear Mr. Obama wants to deploy from Iraq at essentially any risk, under all circumstances within sixteen months, without any perceptible evaluation or delay—but he has also stated that if necessary, he would be willing to return there and that is also fact… *"…but he never talks about winning the war, only ending it."—John McCain—Fox News Online, July 21, 2008.* So why leave until you can guarantee the job is done? I'm sorry Senator, but I just don't see the logic of that, given the above examples I've cited from our Vietnam War withdrawal.

Like many, Obama has been wrong on the War on Terror, his Iraq stance, and particularly the Surge issue. To quote Mr. Continetti again of the Weekly Standard:

"The far-left argued military power would be ineffective against the terrorists. Wrong. It argued that intervention in Iraq would energize bin Laden's movement. That movement is in shambles. The left argued Iraq was a lost cause. It isn't. The left argues that a "war on terrorism" is futile, that defeat is inevitable, because terrorism is a "tactic", not an enemy. Nonsense." –Matthew Continetti—Weekly Standard, June 9th, 2008

So have I at least made enough of a persuasive argument that withdrawal would prove disastrous from the standpoint of the future safety of all Americans, Democrats, Republicans, Independents, and Libertarians alike? I certainly hope so.

And further, I am sick and tired of hearing this conflict referred to as "Bush's War." And while we're at it, let's drop the highly unfair and emotionally charged—"Bush lied...people died" commentary as well.

I am reminded that some great Democratic leaders like Bill Clinton, Al Gore, Hillary Clinton, (and their CIA head; George Tenet), John Kerry, Nancy Pelosi and of course Ted Kennedy all saw the 'Intel' on the Iraqi threat. They too have publicly all proclaimed that they believed that Saddam had W.M.D. and was a danger to the world at large as a result! Perhaps the strongest argument on this issue though comes from the knowledge that the UN itself, had already tried to force Saddam's hand with over a dozen resolutions to get him to surrender his W.M.D. and/or to cooperate with UN inspectors! So let's stop putting this solely in W's court alone...*all of our leaders had lousy intelligence, case closed!* I for one am sick and tired of all the partisan politics and rhetoric.

And here's another pet peeve I have. It seems that one of the most obvious consequences of the growth of the worldwide web is that many surfers have lost not only their sense of humanity, but certainly their manners as well in the process. The degree of blogisphere-based anti-Bush and anti-war vitriol is not only unprecedented—I fear it contains the seeds of anarchy if left unchecked—honestly!

Simply said, this is a war against all Americans and *we must all win it*! Let's allow history to evaluate George W. Bush's judgment without our varied and emotionally charged often-biased input. We have bigger fish to fry now!

In the final analysis, 'W' will go down simply as the opening pitcher in a likely long, Holy War! A trying war with many peaks and valleys, hits and misses, and losses and wins. Frankly, given everything we now know about the intentions of our enemy, it is more likely that 'W's' offensive posture may well prove helpful to our ultimate victory as I've mentioned before—so let's hold judgment ourselves, shall we? And as I've already alluded to; the intentions of this enemy did not begin with 9/11, George Bush's White House, or even with our contemporary foreign policy, so this behaviorist is unwilling to crucify any particular president—until we know more!

Second Impression

Chapter Two

Strange Bedfellows

Where do we look to find the roots of this fanatical ideology in contemporary times? Personally, I for one am saddened that we can't blame it on the explosion of Reality TV programming!

Obsession says we need to look first at the comparables between fundamental Radical Islam and Nazi fascism, in their stated goals, methods, and tactics.

Secondary to methodology, Obsession demonstrates the historical and very real nexus and allied struggle enjoining the former Nazis to their contemporary Arab counterparts. Most notable is the relationship of Hitler and the Grand Mufti of Jerusalem, the religious leader of the Palestinian and Arab National Movement of that era.

The seeds of evil that began with the relationship of these two 'party-poopers', I believe still has relevance today in this conflict, as you will see. Hitler may have burned outside his bunker in 1945, but his dreams and the secret he shared with the Grand Mufti on November 28th, 1941—lives on today in the Middle East! Hitler shared his plans you see, to exterminate all of Europe's Jews, and that was certainly not lost on this Arab cleric. I'm confident that the Mufti and his fellow radical Palestinians of the time, along with the fundamental Arab world at large, so deeply embraced anti Semitism, and the idea of a Jew-free world, that they never forgot or gave up this lofty goal of their German mentor, der fuhrer and how frightening is that?

Naturally, most moderate and liberal Muslims, Palestinians among them, are not only tolerant; they want peace with everyone...Israel included!

Remember that I am only speaking of those fanatical Palestinians and fundamental Islamo Fascists that yet today, share this evil religious ideology. These are the descendents of those same radical fundamentalists! These same Palestinian leaders refused a two-state solution with Israel in 1948 in the first place! Naturally, when the victors of WWII still chose to give the surviving European Jews back their biblical homeland—they knew full well without a two-state solution, it would greatly destabilize the entire Middle East... indefinitely...and it has.

Sadly today in the present Palestinian territory, Hamas legitimately controls Gaza, while the somewhat more moderate Fatah Palestinian movement controls the West Bank...by possession. The unique chess game movements between Hamas vs. Fatah within the Palestinian territory, illustrates perfectly the greater chaos of the region...no one seems to be able to get along peacefully with anyone—for very long.

Hamas is the most powerful terrorist organization in Palestine; they are to Palestine what Hezbollah represents to Lebanon. Like Hezbollah, they enjoy the backing of Iran and Syria, just as Saddam had backed the Palestinian suicide bombers from Hamas and other factions against Israel. Most troubling is that Hamas has the largest infrastructure within the United States itself—of any terrorist organization, according to Obsession. This is a frightening thought and something that must be eradicated somehow.

But let's get back to the relationship of the Grand Mufti and Hitler and how they forged a seemingly unthinkable alliance according to the documentary.

The old cliché, "Preaching to the Choir", aptly defines the strange partnership of the Grand Mufti of Jerusalem, Haj Amin al-Husseini, and Hitler. Their mutual love affair with each other's anti-Semitic ambitions seems to have begun in the mid thirties, specifically 1936. It was based on a simple premise: ***No ideology other than their two—could exist—they were essentially mutually exclusive.*** Aryans and Arabs...yes, Jews...no. Beyond this, the shared hatred of the Jews was long-lived by both men. Beyond these two of course, many Arab Nationalists and Islamic Fundamentalists went well beyond the Mufti and Hitler in their own hatred of the Jewish people, not unlike millions of otherwise peaceful Germans that did the same during the Nazi years.

Obsession purports that the Grand Mufti was not only a fervent supporter of Hitler; he celebrated the man's goals. In essence, if he could have elected der fuhrer 'camel jockey of the year'—he surely would have, in my opinion. The Mufti is also credited as one of the founders of Islamic Fundamentalism as well, something else to celebrate apparently.

The documentary points out that the Grand Mufti was deeply impressed with Hitler's plans for European Jewry. Hitler for his part volunteered these very secret plans of Jewish genocide freely with the Grand Mufti and already had a massive propaganda effort in place to raise the excitement and assistance of the Arab nations to his cause. Most historians rarely mention this fact about Hitler. One can argue that the same annihilation hopes remain the goal today from the Arab side, but let's stay on point regarding their story.

As it happens, the Grand Mufti agreed to join Hitler's efforts to defeat Germany's enemies. The Mufti personally went to the Balkans on Hitler's behalf and raised an entire SS division of Muslims—and that was just the beginning! According to the movie, this is one of the least known facts discussed by students of the Nazi phenomenon since the war's end. Ultimately in fact, the Grand Mufti would raise several SS divisions for Hitler, all containing Arab mercenaries literally volunteered and brought in from around the Arab world…sound familiar?

Yes, there are obvious similarities in my opinion, between the Mufti's forces that once fought for Hitler, and the contemporary insurgents raised by Al Qaeda—currently fighting in the Iraqi front today! And of course, we now see that the current insurgents in Iraq also include direct proxies of the Iranian government as well as Hezbollah—so what other state-sponsored terrorists will be next?

It is certainly my opinion that of all the lessons the Mufti and his fundamentalist followers learned from the Nazis, none could come close to their use of propaganda with the insidious ideological indoctrination that follows!

The film powerfully shows by actual example, how the contemporary Islamo Fascists have literally stolen their anti-Semitic play book at least, i.e. their propaganda flyers and literature, straight off of the Nazi printing presses of the thirties, the images and subversion is generally identical in nature.

Yet the aspect of Islamic Fascist propaganda and its subversion that so pains me personally, as put forward by the film, is in the faces and the voices of today's Palestinian children in particular. It is clear that the Islamo Fascists have exceeded their Nazi mentors in their indoctrination of their Islamic youth. The very worst offense of all as put forward by this hateful ideology, is in its attack on the sanctity of the innocents, their own children!

"This religion Islam will destroy all other religions through the Islamic Jihad fighters." I would prefer to tell

you that this quotation is from a radical mosque or the rare and uncommon ranting of a mad man locked away in some dank and dark cell. Sadly, according to Obsession, this is quoted directly from Palestinian and Jordanian elementary schoolbooks! Further, it is representative of the lengths these fanatics will go to indoctrinate their own children to the core philosophy of this evil ideology…Jihad for Allah!

Many Western mothers and fathers would ask: How can a mother or father stand idly by and watch their child become sucked into this black hole of hatred? Well first, mom and dad have already been brainwashed too and are therefore victims themselves. Secondly, mom and dad see Shahid (dying for Allah) as genuinely bringing great honor to their family within their culture, so if junior wants to plaster himself into itty-bitty bits inside an Israeli mall on a Sunday afternoon—marvelous! The ensuing paragraphs will also hopefully offer a suitable explanation of the phenomenon, and just how innocent the victim is in this horrible conspiracy played out against them.

We need to spend a fair amount of time on this subject, as it is so important and pervasive. We must address it not only from the position of child abuse itself being levied against the movement's children, but other aspects as well.

As a behaviorist, naturally the first issue that comes to mind for me—is how in hell do we eventually deprogram all of these millions of victims of such an evil ideology—that they have known all of their lives? As a hypnotherapist and behaviorist, I realize the difficulty of the task that lies ahead of us. Given the sheer numbers of these victims, I'd like to know just how we will accomplish this naturally—and if, and only when, we first win this global battle that is looming all around us? Trust me, its not going to be a quick fix. It will likely take more than just the current generation being put through counseling, therapy, and deprogramming, and honestly we must not fail to do so. And naturally, we will all be forced to bare the cost of completing the deprogramming as well!

I wish to mention that the film inferentially lays the case that the indoctrination of these helpless victims has gone on for more than a mere single generation already, so much so that this radical ideology is becoming considered mainstream. I am assuming at least the last two to three generations of these fanatics dating back to the fifties have been fully indoctrinated into this ideology.

Nowhere is this indoctrination problem more prevalent and counterproductive than perhaps in the Palestinian territory. Yet any school (known as a Madrassa in Islam) run in countries under Wahhabi-Sunni Islam influence, which was founded by Muhammad ibn Abd-al-Wahhab, might run a close second. Bin Laden as an example, follows Wahhabi Islam. Sadly, some of these radical Wahhabi Madrassas that have been opened around the world over the years, are today located within the United States and other Western nations and we can't honestly be sure of their number.

Let me deviate from the movie for a brief moment though, to explain just how severe of a problem—deprogramming someone so young can be.

According to the late psychotherapist and hypnotherapist, Dr. John G. Kappas' theory of mind, when we are born, our mind is a blank slate if you will…ready to learn by internalizing everything going on around and within the infant's environment. Other than two fears we're born with, and our imbedded instincts and memories within our super conscious…we take in most everything else as new stimuli. The two fears by the way are a fear of loud noises and the fear of falling.

Over the approximate first four years of life, our mind is empty and ripe for input so it pretty much takes in billions of thought impressions or message units, during these initial years of life quite openly. Since all stimuli are saved within the mind's memory like a giant computer hard drive, the mind does begin to fill up from all of these stimuli. Somewhere around the fifth year, our mind begins to start evaluating *and filtering* these repetitive stimuli for those that it identifies with and recognizes—or **knows**...from the ones it doesn't. Now the incoming impressions and thoughts begin coming through as either **known** bits of informative stimuli...or **unknown**. To the mind which never reasoned before, patterns begin to form and core beliefs take hold within it. The mind begins to identify and associate **'knowns' as positive beliefs,** and **anything 'unknown' as a negative**, and the process is complete by the time most children have lived eight or so years!

The problem of course, is that the Islamics' juvenile programming closely resembles this learning process anyway. Even worse, the mind can literally be convinced that **something bad—is good...and vice versa!** While quite erroneous to be sure, it's still seriously problematic. Another way to think of it is to realize that this is a mind generating its own new belief system. If the mind recognizes something as a known (or in other words good) then to the mind...it is good—case closed! In reality therefore, this 'known' thought impression, can be based on anything from good to—something horribly bad (from a sociological point of view) and the mind would only recognize this 'known' as something good. Once the mind accepts it unconditionally as a belief, nothing else matters to the mind. Naturally, I've just shared the abridged and laymen's version of this theoretical process, but the conclusion is the same...programming or encoding by repetition of horrific messages...will be received **positively** into the mind of the child...as a good thing.

Imagine a Palestinian child, born to fanatical fundamentalist parents. Under the above explanation, this baby is constantly fed the following sample stimuli repetitively from the time they are cognitive. And so you know, I'm using their exact rhetoric, translated into English:

All Jews are born of monkeys and pigs.

Allah demands you wage Jihad against all Jews.

You must slit the throats of all Jews…they must die!

But the greatest glory for you is to die for Allah…for Jihad.

By the time this child is five years old, he or she honestly believes these messages on a conscious level and is embedded into his sub-conscious. To put it bluntly, it is all his or her mind has been programmed to believe…***and know***! **Imagine trying to undo all of that false yet evil programming, all of those lies with their countless reinforcement, it's a daunting job, and we'll have to do it!**

And Obsession itself, very poignantly offers exacting testimony to this indoctrination and abuse of the fanatics' children. I must warn you that in many ways, this specific footage is the most difficult for any Western parent to watch, so be forewarned. The poignancy is brought home mostly through numerous images, yet commentary from the children is also included. When we hear one happy and animated little girl, gleefully asserts that she wants to tell Bush that he is a pig, and further hopes—that he dies, the point is already made. Yet her commentary is not ended before stating with genuine sincerity: Thank you! This is paramount you see to demonstrate she was taught proper and fine manners by her parents, **right along with the hatred and hopes for Bush that went along with learning those good manners!**

Worst of all, these children are bombarded constantly with these fanatical views from everywhere within their environment. These youngest victims are always exposed to it. Even their cartoon characters preach annihilation and hatred of the Jews! The Arab Media, driven and fed by these radical elements, have given Hitler's propaganda strategies—new life and great credence. If not on television, they will surely hear honor stories from their fanatical parents, shared stories on the playground at their radical Madrassas, or from their peers, etc…there is no escaping this indoctrination through these countless reinforcing experiences. Given all of this relentless propaganda…what's a child likely to believe? As stated in Obsession: ***"When you hear the same message, over and over again, it becomes part of the way you see the world."*** Further, the film states prior to this, that: ***"A child is not born hating. A child must be taught to hate, and taught to fear."***

Their indoctrination is relentless, all encompassing, and— painful as it is for me to admit, it's quite effective too. Further exacerbating this problem is human nature itself. Even without overt brainwashing, we humans as a whole have always had a real problem in distinguishing between perception and reality, its part and parcel of the human condition if you will. As humans, we are constantly perceiving thoughts, images, and impressions from within our environment, yet many of us never notice when those perceptions are internalized by us as 'real'. I cannot even begin to share with you how problematic this one issue alone becomes, under this onslaught of propaganda and subversion of the masses. In a way perhaps, perception getting accepted as reality, is further evidence and validation of the plausibility of Dr. Kappas' Theory of Mind, isn't it?

As only one illustration of this problem, think about all of the moderate Muslims in the greater Middle East that are subject to all of this propaganda crap exposed through their media on a daily basis. Even if you're a moderate, peace-loving Muslim, how do you suppose you will begin to view Israel and the West when all you hear and read everywhere is that we are scum, dogs, pigs, the infidels? As sad as it is to admit, perception—can become reality in this environment! Naturally, I recognize and hope that most moderate Muslims would choose not to watch these radical television programs in the first place. Yet is some exposure likely, particularly during the holy month of Ramadan when the family hankers in around the TV, yes it is.

And the real danger of the Arab media's propaganda assault is painfully measurable by the total lack of response to go against it by the International and American mainstream media itself! In my opinion, without some antidotal countermanding commentary by our media to battle the countless lies—what hope do we have of quelling them? In such a one-sided environment, it is next to impossible to affect real change here. **Our media's own stillness therefore, affirms, supports, and enforces the Arab media's propaganda by its silence!**

Yet without proactive change, what hope exists that moderate Muslims have much chance of developing a pro-western empathy of support, let alone a neutral opinion of Israel? As such, the fanatical tirades of the Arab media are becoming accepted and believed throughout the 'main-stream' of the Arab world, and this is our greatest threat! According to the documentary, *"these influences are becoming so mainstream it's frightening"*.

The worst concern I have is that no one to date seems to have any type of estimate on the percentage of the other more moderate Muslims out there. And further, how do we classify those Muslims that already have anti-West and anti-Israel sympathies into the mix of the greater population? Their percentage isn't known and it naturally troubles me as such. Without any idea of the percentage of the moderate Muslim population beyond the 85% left after the radicals are omitted. What's frightening is obvious to many: as we need all remaining moderate Muslims to be our Ambassadors to the rest of the Arab street, so numbers do matter! And what if there are five hundred million (500) more Muslims that fall into that anti-Western category…what then? You see, we really must know the true numbers we're dealing with here!

Given the power of perception and the repetitive nature of this propaganda by the Arab media, is it any wonder why the film would state that: *"Infiltration of radical Islam is so deep…it's shocking.* " At some point, we must ask ourselves honestly: How pervasive is this phenomenon already?

An inkling to the answer perhaps can be drawn from this comment in the documentary:

"While the vast majority of Muslims are peaceful… there are those from within our own country that have already been taught by extremists, in extremist mosques and by extremist tapes, that you can readily get today, to hate the country you live in, and to support only the most extreme elements of radical Islam, dedicated to the destruction of Western values…and that is a serious problem!"

It has been reported that one Islamic Madrassa—**in Virginia**, was found to have textbooks for…their American Islamic students that appear to preach radical ideology! The Islamic Saudi Academy in Virginia appears to be among those American Madrassas funded by the Saudi government through their charities, and influenced by its Wahhabi Islam roots. We will explore this fully in Part Two.

Third Impression

Chapter Three

"No Evil Disappears of It's Own Accord"

It appears from several perspectives, that it's unlikely we will be able to 'luck' our way out of this global threat, it's already too big, serious, and widespread for that. As Obsession so clearly points out: *"It seems that each generation is called upon, to defend liberty at some point."*

It is not surprising with our modern internet-age society with no shortage of sources for our news, that we would view any conflict at least initially with suspicion. The degree of suspicion perhaps parallels the politics of the participant. To be fair, there are multiple ways to look at any given issue or problem.

Here then, we begin with a sample of what the left's more pacifistic approach could look like as a solution to the problem:

Let's walk the high road and just ignore these extremists until they realize we're not so bad…right? Let's try to get along; maybe we should just keep religion out of this? If we sidestep sensitive issues and simply extend the olive branch while reaching out, won't we convince these Islamic patriots that nothing good will come from conflict? Shouldn't we listen to these people, aren't we responsible for their anger towards us after all?

No—No—No—and—No!

Let's take these contemporary 'four questions'—one at a time, shall we?

To begin with, we can ignore these fanatics all we want—but simply said, they're not going anywhere until they have 'Islamosized' the entire planet, a buzzword you'll hear more about later. For now though, think of it like superseding your own religious beliefs as simply as your last fast-food meal was super-sized for a mere 49 cents more! Simply said, nothing else matters to these fanatics' long term goals—for them, Islam must rule the planet. "***They want to replace our constitution—with their Koran!***" You will hear it in their own words—yourself, all you have to do is watch the film, so don't let me sway you.

Secondly, as previously put forward we must not minimize the fact that this is a Holy War. Entranced believers make very passionate warriors, especially those indoctrinated through the leaders and schools of the religion. What part of: "This is a fight to the Death", do we not understand?

From my perspective as a political scientist, only through understanding their religious precepts and laws can we have any hope of swaying moderates outside of their direct influence to consider other peaceful options. And believe me; here we are dealing with an ideology so fundamentally barbaric, so truly antiquated, that their own high clerics proudly display their sabers openly to their congregations in abhorrent testimony to their God and his prophet's violent beliefs.

For Muslim moderates, we must expose the failings of the fanatics' extremism through an aggressive dialogue. A conversation that puts forth, argues for, and lays a testament to the modern alternative, that of a peaceful loving version of Islam.

The problem of course, is that if you really study Islam through the Koran and Haditha, and in particular—their glorious prophet Mohammad, you see that this singular Islamic icon was not the most peace-loving fellow out there... not hardly! He apparently started out peaceful in Mecca, but as he became powerful, wealthy, and a warlord in Medina...he changed dramatically.

Taken literally on face value sadly, the Prophet's teachings and interpretations cannot be called peaceful, and one would have to argue if being intellectually honest therefore, that Islam itself, in its true yet fundamental interpretations, is a religion that promotes at times, a violent discourse!

Now ask yourself the painful question here, accordingly. If the above is true...which is the true and real Islam? The peaceful version practiced by millions of moderate Muslims, or the violent foundations followed by the terrorists? I hate to say it, because I am neither a religious scholar nor expert, but I vote for the latter!

Third—terrorists...especially those who will conduct war against their own moderate people, believe appeasement offered by its foes is something that is to be exploited and encouraged and yet ultimately...conquered! These warriors are only going to respond to strength.

Understand something—this is an opponent who prays to die! Your only course of action with that type of warrior—is a 100% defeat or destruction of their forces!

Perhaps here is a most poignant current example, as writing any book continues as a work in progress until it's finished. The date is May 21st, 2008, and today the Parliament of Lebanon may have laid its own seeds of ultimate defeat against terrorism by acquiescing to Hezbollah's demands for a greater number of seats within their own Parliament.

The head of Lebanon's army failed to defend the country against Hezbollah's strong-arm tactics, and now he is in line to be appointed the country's next president...what a surprise! Remember only time will tell, yet this much is true, another puppet government run by a terrorist organization was born today, as we will learn from Part Two!

And finally, why would we listen to these zealots lie to us? They hate everything we represent and honor. As such, we are their punching bag as their contrived enemy, thoroughly orchestrated, propagandized, and marketed as effectively as any Coca Cola product launch! According to their leaders, we are responsible for essentially every negative social problem facing the region including not being able to attract a spouse! We simply represent the excuse they have created as the justification for their calls for self-preservation through Jihad. It's a control mechanism over the masses of their fundamental followers, who would otherwise turn against—them for their own pathetic, poor, and terrible lives.

So despite what our compassionate peace loving, left-leaning friends would say, we simply cannot ignore the risks that the verbalized threats and vitriol of the players within this conflict represent and are putting forward. Players such as Iran's Ahmadinejad is a perfect example, he is presenting not only rhetoric within his incendiary comments...but laying out the group's actual plans and wishes!

I'm reminded of my friendly chiding of Senator Obama earlier for claiming he was right about Iraq perhaps prematurely. After all, looking back **seventy years** to Adolf Hitler—were his rants within his verbalized threats and vitriol—brag...or fact? Were they empty threats...or stated, yet unrealized goals of the Nazi movement? ***"If we fail to learn from history, we are destined to relive it."*** So says Obsession—so says...me.

So can we afford to just wait this out—not likely? The problem is not going away, and the attacks will continue, as the rhetoric itself becomes elevated and self-fulfilling, and the actions of those within these radical Islamic communities around the world, will likely become bolder, if not in scale... than in frequency! What's more in my opinion, is the longer we deny the problem and put off the inevitable conflict, the weaker we will be perceived by them and increase the risks as they become more emboldened. Here's how I see the conflict moving forward.

First, we had better get ready for an even longer conflict and wider war on expanded fronts, so large that perhaps the necessity to reawaken a conscription military will be necessary if a surge of volunteers is insufficient on its own, although we may have plenty of them.

And we will not be in this expanded conflict alone either. This time we will enjoy our largest coalition ever, far beyond our war in Afghanistan or the first Gulf War. Why you ask? Because most countries around the world will have sadly realized by then that they must join the fight with us, to hopefully survive the threat. And we'll need every ally, even though many will have little to offer...but moral support and a little money!

This is post-modern warfare, with no rules honored by our enemy. So no abuse by our enemy against our innocent citizens proves too brash or outrageous, the more brazen the better!

Horrific warfare will likely ensue that initially we are totally unprepared for. At first the terror will frighten us, as the audacity eventually angers us. Thankfully, the experience will transform us! We will unite, perhaps as strongly as 1776 honestly and truly recognize our shared humanity!

Americans will have witnessed a warfare where five-year-old babies are strapped with plastic explosives and sent into our unsuspecting public locations...and then detonated by remote control. Our enemy will expect us to weep for our fallen countrymen...yet we cry foremost for that innocent little baby whose life was stolen.

When this conflict is in full swing, we are going to have to pit our technology and creativity against their own creativity, brawn, improvisation, absence of decency, biologics, and suicide-bombing audacity. They will rely upon their network of cell structures and shadow communities, embedded in countries around the world and their support system of fundamental Islamic nations and their friends. I fear candidly, that Part Two of this book may prove painful to some of us.

On their 'A' list for primary financial support, are Iran, Saudi Arabia, Syria, and many of their individual warriors come from their puppets—Lebanon and Palestine and various other groups too.

On the 'B' list of ancillary, sympathetic, and/or technical support nations, are OPEC exporter Venezuela, Cuba, and North Korea. North Korea as an example, supplied the technology to Syria for their nuclear reactor. Other supporters will surprise some of you, while still other players such as Russia...should be watched closely with their support of Iran. No fringe organizations should be above reproach. Domestic gangs, drug lords and their cartels, and sympathetic Islamic brotherhood organizations located domestically—and in foreign countries as well.

Allow me to offer a fundamental truth as paraphrased from Obsession to close this chapter:

"Ultimately the price we're talking about is the price of freedom. In every generation I think, at some point, we are called upon to defend our freedom, at that juncture—we must stand up for that ideal."

I for one look forward to us doing that as a united country once again.

Next Impression

Chapter Four

PC Might Well Be The Scourge of Our Times

A Case For Why Political Correctness Must End!

I'm all for being polite to everyone, regardless of race, gender, sexual preferences, etc. I personally like and appreciate gentility, kindness, and sensitivity expressed outwardly to all, I truly do. That being said, as a Behaviorist—here is my brief argument against Political Correctness paranoia as currently being worshipped by some.

When we become so self-constrained in taking legal, logical steps and actions, and compromise our nation's own National Security or safety as a result...I will always side with protecting our country and ourselves first. Let the PC politeness be damned! You see, when our nation's security efforts are allowed to be compromised in the all-important work of keeping our citizens safe by how and those we profile—just to promote proper PC...something has gone horribly wrong with the way we perceive the value gained! We must still defend logic and set realistic priorities. Peace after all—is a far greater virtue than politeness—and defending our country's freedoms—greater still. Politeness pales in importance when compared to safeguarding one's country. Which of these possible two outcomes presents the more compelling and important principle value to our American society and humanity at large?

Our first outcome, protected some of our country's minorities—multiple ethnicities of persons of middle eastern appearance traits, from undue scrutiny and embarrassment at JFK and other airports—accomplished by being hyper sensitive and careful not to over profile them with focused TSA security screening.

Our second outcome results in potentially insulting, upsetting, and possibly even traumatizing those same airplane passengers who fit one of many profiles of possible terrorists. This action however, leads to the arrest of a suicide bomber/terrorist boarding a packed flight of nearly four hundred people, from New York to Los Angeles with undetected plastic explosives!

Honestly friends—which outcome is likely to protect the greater good from a purely mathematical and societal point of view...and when does—nice manners and sensitivity—trump 400 innocent lives? Which principle is more important to you and your family? (Either inside or outside of those 400 saved victims.)—I know where I stand.

Let's face it, there are simply appropriate times when our desire to uphold PC must be compromised for the greater good...and safety of an entire country of 300 million people. And our own press media needs to remember and adhere to this too.

Look and consider what's happening with this Holy War and its players, is there any doubt as to why our own media—too often, remain silent—when they shouldn't? Of course not. You see, looked at from another perspective, **our media is petrified to be seen by the Muslim community— as responsible** for exposing what is happening with this conflict...Heaven help them—Allah forbid.

My argument simply contends that there will be plenty of time for apologies and reconciliation after we save the world from this global threat! That being said, any other approach to dealing with a threat of this magnitude is foolhardy indeed.

In closing my argument, I would simply say that before Political Correctness stands in the way of preserving our country's safety—**it** must be sacrificed...**before all Americans including you and I!**

Obsession makes it clear that we are: **"strangling ourselves with our political correctness"**, I agree, and would add that we need to be more vigilant and more demanding of our media. While Obsession makes a compelling case that we are all living in denial here in the West, I sadly have a somewhat different spin on this issue.

It seems to me that in order for a society itself to be in denial over an issue they first must have a working knowledge of the issue itself. If so few even know about the issue...how can they be in denial in the first place?

While most Americans will acknowledge that they are clear who the combatants are in this 'War on Terror', the vast majority do not seem to have a handle on the breadth and seriousness of the conflict...and the consequences of losing this war—nor that it's a single global war. If they did, I find it simply impossible to believe that levelheaded, reasonable, and freedom-loving Americans would risk the future of this country's freedoms and liberties so casually by blowing out of Iraq or anywhere else—prematurely. The blame for this lack of knowledge of the American people lies solidly in the lap of the American Press Media!

Honestly folks, this war has a disconnect with the American people right now, much to the lack of efforts put forward by a flippant, bias, and PC-phobic press media, so much so, I refer to it as: ***The Unintended, Intentional Media Blackout!*** Our press has taken a very cavalier and stupid position, one full of indifference and failure to report the facts at the expense of their own safety…let alone the rest of us.

The press should have been all over this global threat more than five years ago…yes I said five long years ago! When you watch Obsession, you will see actual scenes of hundreds of thousands of radical Islamic Fascists calling for Death to America at super huge rallies—carried by the Arab Media! You will see young children call for death to the Jews. You realize that these films do not appear out of thin air—they're recorded and filmed, and copies are available for review by the entire world's press for countless years to follow their original broadcast.

The hate propaganda against the West is so pervasive that it is now mainstream in the Arab World. Yet in the Western world; the fundamental Islamists through their representatives, put out a far different persona…literally a brazenly disingenuous PR campaign. They preach tolerance, peacefulness, and universal values…and to my way of thinking…none of it rings true. I do not believe it is sincere when you can read from their Koran and see what their followers do, that this can be a religion of peace…sorry, but this old coot isn't buying a word of it, it is deception—pure and simple…and we had better wake the hell up while we still can.

And of course, our press eats it all up, so do our leaders, because no one wants to be accused of being racist or unPC! Where is our Press Media's backbone, disbelief, and shock? Where is their effort…their defense and a call to action?

Why isn't our press splashing this all over our own American TVs? There is a simple reason beyond these PC aspects. And all I can say is—his name is George W. Bush!

Our press has decided by itself—that it won't report the truth about this threat and the full facts of the Iraq war either, because if they did...they would ultimately be forced to admit something painfully accurate and profound. And all it comes down to is a simple acknowledgment...that *George W. Bush's actions were proven prudent!*

The press realizes that if they were to do some honest reporting and investigate the actions of these radical Islamic Fascists fully, they would be forced to vindicate the President's insistence on waging this war—directly to the American people. This confession would naturally be so totally deplorable and vile to the American Press Media...as it is—long overdue, so they are avoiding it like the plague. For the Press to eat crow and admit that despite how we may have entered the war, or the shortcomings of our initial reasons, the threat now fully exposed by this war presents this as a valid conflict—one that is extremely necessary. The result of such a confession would destroy our press' very biased agenda so they won't go down that road under any circumstances!

So we are forced to accept that our Press Media will not be candid and honest with us! And for little more justification than protecting their own bruised egos and biases therefore... *today every American is at a greater risk of harm from these Islamic fanatics!* So who do you think we should thank first for aiding and abetting...and bringing comfort to our enemies—I ask you?

We have discussed how perception can become reality through repetitious indoctrination, so I hope you realize that what befalls the goose will sink the gander as well? Americans are just as susceptible to believing anything our media says and reports, or doesn't report in our case, as are these radicals from their Arab TV's propaganda.

A perfect example of 'perception rules' can be seen by interviewing any number of thousands of Democrats who were the most ardent supporters of the Clinton administration and drank the press' main perception that flowed freely over the post-Clinton years.

If you ask these supporters of the Clintons, what was the most important accomplishment of these two administrations from 1992-2000, they will proudly tell you that President Clinton's two administrations brought to the American people...Peace and shared Prosperity in the 1990's. Now while we can all agree that the Clinton years were prosperous for the country, there were some outside factors beyond the White House involvement as well, but let's not argue that point, let's give the man his due. Where I really take issue with this perception and declare it as erroneous, is in discussing the issue of 'Peace' itself during this Clintonian period of contemporary history.

Let's see—we had the first attack on the WTC in 1993. Following that was the Khobar towers bombings, the USS Cole, our embassies in Kenya and Tanzania—with many linked directly to Bin Laden and all to terrorist factions. These are only some of the more infamous attacks all falling under Mr. Clinton's watch—and what did he do about any of it? Oh yes, he bombed an aspirin factory, I nearly forgot. ***When offered Bin Laden on a silver platter by Sudan five years prior to 9/11,*** our illustrious leader at that juncture was rumored to have told the Sudanese: "I don't know what to charge him with, you'd better keep him". That's how focused Mr. Clinton was on the terrorist threats during his presidency...so he gets no pass or acclaim from this old conservative. Conversely, this threat to our existence has been so cloistered in secrecy by our enemies and misunderstood, I will not blame President Clinton either...beyond his lack of action. Sorry but I won't go there. What I will say is that:

President Clinton mostly ignored all of these threats; swept them under the rug, labeled them criminal issues—not the terrorist attacks that they were, and the Press Media—simply gave him a pass over it. They more than any other, created and perpetuated the 'perception' of peace during those eight years—and what a crock of crap that it all was! Between 1992 and 2000, we had over six thousand injured, and an excess of four hundred murdered…under his administrations' watch. The press apparently is willing to forget Rwanda and Somalia, the USS Cole and Khobar Towers…well I'm not! So you see, the Clintonian years were far from…peaceful and free of victims of terrorism! Yet according to some, only Bush's policies created victims that died! Gee, so who lied this time?

I am of the opinion that this false reporting or creative broadcasting by the media, is in its own right, a form of propaganda, in and of itself, intentional or otherwise, and I welcome a journalist to debate me on the subject! Now let's move on to Washington.

For some unknown reason, our White House itself has to date, failed to call this war…a Holy War, something it truly is, and somehow this troubles me on many levels.

My first inclination, closely aligned with my behaviorist roots, is that the government is potentially hiding something from us so insidious or menacing; we would simply not be able to handle it, so the prez and possibly the press are aligned in silence to protect us.

Yet there is another possibility, another point to consider far less ominous, and that is that the President by nature, is likely most comfortable keeping the conflict in simple terms and more secular and political, then to call it by its truthful name. Obviously a Holy War where our enemy seeks the 100% destruction of our civilization and everything we stand for in the name of God…certainly their God. It just doesn't give us all a warm and fuzzy like watching American Idol—now does it?

President Bush must be of the opinion that our allies and potential allies, but certainly all of us, can only be sold so much at one time. I'm reminded here of that wonderful movie 'What About Bob?' and those necessary 'baby steps'.

As an informed society however, we have to be able to depend on the watchdog elements within our country to function well and transparently during wartime. In this light, I must return to our media's manifest role within our society for this responsibility.

We have to be able to count on honesty of our press media at all times, as our 'eyes' out there behind enemy lines, keeping us informed and in the know. Based on those simple responsibilities I am very angry indeed at our Press Media. How as an example, could all of this hate propaganda against the United States, go so completely unreported by the American media for these many years...even prior to 9/11? It's absurd to debate it.

As a nation under the cloud of war, we are entitled to an honest press, case closed. As an American, I'm so disappointed in our contemporary media and their handling of the whole sorted affair I'm at a loss to even suggest a solution. I believe we deserved much better from our press than we got...and now we're all going to suffer because of the deceit they have perpetuated against us, for all these years!

I am firmly convinced that some of the actions of our Press Media are certainly guilty of gross negligence of their fiduciary responsibilities to their fellow American citizens. Perhaps too, there are some whose actions border on treasonous acts. I have no desire to research it deeper now, as I fear the possible results would only upset me further.

One need only look at the facts: Sparse reporting when the facts were positive, as opposed to massive coverage when the news was negative on the war. At best, its inaccurate, biased, and falsely focused coverage. Hell it doesn't take much to realize—I've made my case already!

Beyond our Press Media, I must not fail to mention some other apparent champions of defeat, redeployment, and naysaying. Before I do though, I apologize beforehand. You see, I've tried to keep this book as neutral as possible. Yet here, if I don't speak my peace on this subject, how am I to look myself in the mirror in the morning? It would be disingenuous of me, so as I've already said, please accept my apology if I'm a little brusque here. But you see, there are outspoken Members within both houses of Congress and they're primarily Democrats, frankly and I honestly feel that their vitriol and divisive commentary was very counterproductive to our Military's brilliant performance and damning to their morale, which is where my real disappointment in these leaders is rooted. In this regard, they were of no help to our country and during a time of war, I feel it was inappropriate and sad.

These great Americans are the supposed leaders of their party. Yet when they couldn't keep quiet, and insisted on insulting everything from our collective bad intelligence to the progress and behavior of the war and our troops, I frankly lost some respect for them. From their inaccurate finger pointing, accusations, and verbal slander—to downright insults, these passionate objectors have given new meaning to the word liberal **and deplorably—all during a time of war!**

How can we ever forget Harry Reid's wonderful commentary last year, when he purported in the chambers of the United States Senate, that: "The surge has failed, the war is lost". And lest we forget Congressional Committee Chairman, Jack Murtha's comments when he began implying our military were murdering innocent people in Haditha!

It's a funny thing though…as each important Surge milestone was reached within Iraq since reaching full-force; these same leaders have had several bouts of selective amnesia it seems. They were forever moving the goal posts further back with each success, in a vain attempt to save face with

America, yet most Americans now see them for what most of them are…**defeatists!**

First, some of these members of Congress bet the farm early on, that the Iraq surge and the war in general would end in defeat. Now that it hasn't *gone that way*…which is to say…*failed*—they're trying to make the case that the war is just too expensive to continue to fight any longer! I believe this idiocy was exemplified best by more than a few members ranting: *"We cannot win this war militarily"* (…*even as we were!*) This theme was repeated by numerous members within Congress and at the expense of the morale and safety of our Military risking their lives daily.

To the argument of defeatism, I would personally respond: *"We have a very dangerous enemy out there…and we need to grow up quick…kiss and make-up…and face this thing…united." Mitch Reed, O.O.O.—2008*

From the beginning, many of us on the right suspected we would see a few Democrats to put their eggs into the basket of defeat, failure, and bashing the administration…and it's their right to do so. One would think though—that they had no say in voting to go to war—and perhaps they want you to forget that little fact…*that they did!*

Before we begin Part Two of this book, may I suggest that its time for a seventh-inning stretch. Put down the book for a spell and watch and share this documentary yourselves…do it now, why don't you? It will be an important first step in your own awakening. Go to www.obsessionthemovie.com if you haven't done so already.

PART TWO

Predictions, Consequences, and Strategies From My Perspective

"Denial is not a defense…it's a Death Sentence"—
Author

In the twenty some odd years preceding 9/11, we experienced over 7,500 acts of terror around the globe…is someone trying to get our attention, maybe!

Chapter Five

What Happens If We Lose?
Predicting the Consequences of Defeat

What follows here is conjecture, and certainly most of my opinions are not derived from Obsession for this second section. I believe however, that this is the appropriate placement within the book for this chapter, as after all, what follows is not a guaranteed prediction, but rather the likely consequences. As I see it, you need to know what we are fighting to protect, beyond our mere existence.

If the United States and its coalition partners were to lose this battle, you have a right to know what daily life in America would be like—but where do I begin?

We could start with the primary focus of this enemy's goals. Those of us that do survive will no longer be free to practice the religion of our own choosing or faith…all other religions will be forbidden, outlawed! You will be like an indentured servant to the Islamic faith, and forced to accept the faith and practice it passionately, or face very nasty consequences and second-class status! Continual kidnappings, beheadings, and other 'tools' will likely be used to break our spirits and to keep us in tow…and fear.

Any surviving Jews would likely be put to death while imprisoned…as a second holocaust on religious principle—or enslaved, if among the lucky 'needed' Jews.

Women will have all of the restrictions placed upon them as any woman already faces daily, in radical Middle Eastern countries. They will wear no make up, and since forced to wear a burka covering their faces, they really won't need Revlon or Cosmo any longer anyway. And not to belabor the point, but they won't have anything to say about it any old how.

You see, women will be subjugated thoroughly as second-class citizens and not allowed to make their own basic decisions; those will all be relegated to their fathers, husbands, or brothers, including the selection of their husbands! Ladies…are you listening to this crap?

Our children will only reside with us for basic shelter and sustenance, their indoctrination and upbringing will be solely in the hands of the Imams while—their loyalty will exclusively be bound to Allah—by more fear of death! And remember these are our babies…our children!

The indoctrination of our children will be centered within their schooling at the local little red Madrassa where they will learn a wide curriculum of fabulous Islamic subjects such as: Bomb-making 101, You and your AK47, Jew-sightings and other UFO's, Internet Terrorism 101 & 102, Husbands Know Best, Modern Martyrdom, and—Good Mosque keeping.

And don't worry, your children will be very busy with numerous after school activities too…lots of target practice for one thing, and with live targets. Learners' permits will be traded in for bomb-making practice and assault exercises, better than any X box game you could create, believe me! If they excel here, (by surviving) likely they will be invited to

Abdullah's Terrorist Camp for Discriminating Teens...to wile away their summer vacations and all weekends. If all goes well there, they will rise to the top of their Allah Youth Movement platoon...earning their own C4 (plastic explosive) and Koran during Ramadan.

Our kids will hardly notice the loss of their secular music, cell phones, I-pods, video games, and hanging at the mall... they're just going to love these small adjustments—aren't they?

All travel will have to be approved. The press and all media will be under Islamic guidelines, and all decisions must meet the percepts of Islam and will be approved by your local Imam.

All material possessions naturally will be shunned and avoided under penalty of death. The sole exception will likely be your car...but it's a double-edged sword. Yes, you can still have a Mercedes in their world...but your wife won't be licensed to drive it, so with the absence of sex that result from that one fiasco alone, no one smiles much...or gets laid ever again!

In all seriousness, as Americans, we have always been in the unique position to have never been under a victor's rule before. As material as we all can be, that's probably a good thing. Sadly though, that will make our pain of being under Islamic rule—that much more difficult as an adjustment. Life under Islam is not merely a religion that one takes personally like other faiths; Islam is an all-encompassing religious and political system absorbing you into its non-negotiable shariah laws and existence! One lives by Islam, he doesn't practice it!

We will literally be a conquered society that previously was freedom-based and the adjustment will be nearly impossible to overcome. Yet for the first time in our history, others will tell us what to eat, what to drink...and lo—not to drink, and we thought Prohibition was tough!

The fruits of our labors and technology will be obediently turned over to our religious leaders, as we are incapable of determining their worth to Allah by ourselves. In fact, we're not trusted to do anything by ourselves. We will be instructed as to who we will help, who we will oppose, who we can even speak to.

Those of us that cooperate with our captors, will enjoy special privileges—including two extra virgins when we die; Fatima and Sharma and get to meet Allah personally which should be at the ripe old age—of 54 when adjusted for the mass suicides that will follow living under Islamic conquest!

And of course, the end of American Jewry as we know it will bring its own set of unexpected consequences. Most evident will be the total collapse of the Medical industry, as there will be no Board-Certified Physicians left to treat the sick. Overnight, golf courses will go broke, Lexus dealers will close their doors, and Pakistani doctors will be swamped and forced to stop taking on new patients altogether.

Mixed opinions will ensue though, over the consequences of the collapse of our entire American Legal system too. You see, it will dawn on the entire country more-or-less... simultaneously—that there are few lawyers left alive—to sue these Islamo bastards in the first place!

Mass depression will also result from the realization that the entire entertainment industry and its infrastructure was Jewish...who knew? Gone too are the writers, directors, producers, etc. to create a single worthwhile program or piece of film. Of course this will have no effect on the propagation of the Arab Media and their 'reality' programming being forced into our lives—will it? Oh joy!

Equally painful are the losses to the worlds of Art, Music, Science, and not to underestimate this impact—to the Comedy Club circuit. And don't even get me started on how unhappy the country will become when they realize that for once they have to figure out their own taxes...oy gavalt!

Yes, the void left behind by this insignificant 2% of our country's population, now seems so disproportionate and a great loss to our American way of life indeed…oy vay (that's a double oy gavalt!).

In essence my fellow Americans, nothing will be the same for us. A great and diverse country founded on personal freedoms will be stripped of those rights, and our country will cease to exist as it has for some two hundred and thirty two years. Nothing will feel right…or American any longer. And how sad we will all be over that sole realization alone.

With the possible exception of a few Americans who may find a certain vindication in our defeat and suffering, and likely celebrate the changes as uplifting, refreshing—and invigorating, yet for most Americans we will feel very low indeed. Allah…friggin'…Akbar!

Naturally, once we have been defeated, our new leaders will find good use of all our accumulated Military power too—finishing the rest of the planet off as well. And with all of our children so thoroughly trained now on the art of suicide bombing by remote control detonation, they have short—but very bright futures ahead of them within the American Islamic Revolutionary Guard—don't they? So when conscription returns down the road…think about this alternative before you send junior packing for Canada!

Yet personally, I believe the very worst stab into our hearts will be something so simple and taken for granted, we barely even noticed it until we lost it!

Sadly…we may never know peace again…in our time!

Chapter Six

Our Current Status

We Can't Win...If We Don't Engage

Here is our current situation as I see it, and in continuing this second component of the book—let me boldly state unequivocally:

We are currently winning this war at least on the Iraqi front. This is sadly at the expense of all of the naysayers out there who said we could never win.

By almost any measurement, the real facts in Iraq do not lie, nor do they herald the negativity continuing to be put forward by our friends—the naysayers and here's how I see their conundrum in particular.

I believe that some on the left have become more invested in the war's failure than its success, since it was determined way back when, that no W.M.D.'s were going to be found. This single fact became simply reprehensible and unimaginable for these passionate patriots to accept. And I could have done without their antipathy, the likes of which particularly on the blogs, I have never seen in modern American times. Beyond that—it became a turning point and a call to arms for the anti-war warriors, if you will.

As a behaviorist, I would say these war opponents became so emotionally fixated on that error in our faulty domestic and military intelligence, that they could not maintain their objectivity. So for them at that moment, it became all about Bush's rush to an unjustified war. Bush to many of these loyal Americans had only recently stolen the American Presidency from Mr. Gore.

Naturally, those on the left were justifiably still upset with '*W*' to begin with and the Intel fiasco didn't help. The left's new mantra: ***Bush lied, and people died***—battle cry was born.

The opponents of this conflict can only guide their efforts on one principle motivation—above all others—***We must withdraw and remove our troops—yesterday, because the bastard lied to us about why we had to go to war in the first place...so no other justification matters to us...let's just get us the hell out!***

The vast majority of Americans have moved past this issue, understanding the intelligence was flawed ***by several sources***, and put forward—flawed, and then shared with all major leaders and players within the executive and legislative branches of our government. Those Americans that remain vehemently against the President—for whatever their reasons...have not! To them, the viable solution to such a betrayal is withdrawal and redeployment.

Don't get me wrong, the left has a very valid argument to make concerning how this conflict has distracted us away from the earlier Afghanistan front, and that is a fair point in my opinion. After all, I keep touting this is one global war, don't I?

In hindsight—perhaps Iraq was not the next logical front. I think we can all agree that Iran today poses a very challenging threat to the world in general, and not only to the region. Did we play into the Iranian's hands by going into Iraq ourselves first—yes we did! Anyone who would deny this fact is just as erroneously fixated as any on the left. My fellow compassionate conservatives simply mouthing the Administration's talking points aren't any better in my opinion than the complaints and vitriol coming from our friends on the left.

But back in Iraq, I am pleased to say however, that as of late, Al Qaida is in a state of disarray, at least for the moment. There in Iraq, they are all but absent except in Mosul.

In Iraq, there is reason for some much-needed optimism. It appears that a refocused Nuri Al-Maliki government, along with a revitalized Iraqi army, is greatly bolstered by much of this change, along with the Iraqi people themselves. The Iraqi civilians became fed up with Al Qaida and their severe and horrific tactics, and have therefore embraced our troops and turned against Al Qaida for the most part.

And where all of us go wrong in my opinion however, is in failing to recognize the significance of our involvement in Iraq, or anywhere else…from the 'Holy Jihad' perspective. From that vantage point, it matters not how we got there at all…like to Iraq vs. Iran vs. wherever. Had similar flawed intelligence led us into Pakistan or Iran for instance, we would still be fighting *the same essential war* now folks, albeit with different variables and dynamics. We really need to wake up to this fact. Repeat after me: The war is global, only the fronts will change!

To repeat guys—this is one global war with numerous fronts, and so we need to take the macro view here. According to Obsession again, we are at war with a religious ideology that has a foothold in **58 state countries!** And we now know so much more.

How will they infiltrate you ask?   Through the establishment of shadow communities around the world... including in the US, now let me share a recent article with you. According to Amir Taheri in the New York Post, **he speaks of a new playbook of sorts by Al Qaeda's chief theoretician, Sheik Abu-Bakar Naji.** Naji's new book is titled: "Governance in the Wilderness—Taheri states in his article that: *"There is a Plan B Manifesto out there." –Amir Taheri, July 2, 2008 New York Post.*

Does that mean that fifty-eight (58) potential fronts already exist to launch fights and aggression from around the globe, quite possibly...yes! So does it make a rat's ass difference from that perspective—where in those 58 states—we enter the fight...of course not? In Arabic, these potential shadow communities are called Edarat al-Wahsh which literally means: Governance in the Wilderness.

It would appear that this enemy plans to defeat us by infiltrating us from the inside out...one country at a time! This is scary sh_t. But let's get back to the Iraq front, for a moment, shall we?

Thanks to General Patraeus' surge strategy, the commitment, and training of our brilliant troops, and of course President Bush's openness to change a stagnant strategy in Iraq, the situation has dramatically improved since last fall on this current front. And the Iraqi government is finally stepping up to the plate on meeting Congress' eighteen milestones, to begin the reconciliation, wealth sharing, and bringing the rogue militias under control. We are seeing dramatic improvements almost daily. US casualties are down dramatically over 80% and the reductions in Iraqi casualties mirror that.

Yet as we see these improvements in Iraq...notice now the resurgence of the Taliban in Afghanistan...so you see, we truly are fighting a very motivated and resilient enemy fighting one global battle...aren't we? Remember, Jihad literally translated means to struggle within. Part of that struggle is certainly physical, and assuredly part of it must be spiritual in order to look 'within'. As a behaviorist, I believe what makes Jihad so important and consuming to Islamist fundamentalists is that while fighting for Allah; struggle can embody both aspects of Jihad simultaneously, making it a desirable experience as a spiritual awakening to the Jihadist in question. Also realize something very crucial to looking at Islam...there is no guaranteed salvation if you will, such as in Christianity. So the next best thing is Mohammad's teachings in the Haditha, where he alludes to reaching martyrdom by Shahid, and going to paradise as a reward. Translation: To be assured of immortality, die for Allah!

So what about Afghanistan and Iraq you ask? Well with General Patraeus' recent promotion to commander of operations at Central Command for the entire region, I am confident the improvements he has brought to Iraq with his counterinsurgency strategy there, can be successfully adapted for our continuing fight in Afghanistan, where coalition forces continue to fight an energized and revitalized Taliban...yet again.

And in Iraq, positive changes do continue, not the least of which is the final absence of Saddam Hussein's reign of terror! Real freedoms are taking hold, as a vibrant young country emerges out of a repressed fog—and a modern economically sound democracy appears on the horizon.

Please understand something critical here as well. **What is happening in Iraq is a true beacon to the rest of the oppressed peoples of the region...those <u>moderate</u> Sunni's, Shiites, Arabs, and Farsi. A place, where quite honestly, moderate Muslims in particular can look and evaluate for themselves, who is offering more hope and solutions for their problems...the West...or those radical Imams?**

I also believe that moderate Arab countries as well as Israel, will welcome a re-invigorated Iraq into the region's family of nations with support, trade, and assistance. So with each success we achieve in Iraq, the greater argument we can present to the peoples of the Middle Eastern region...to wit: Which future do you wish to see for your country...and your lives?

Don't be misled by anyone...victory in Iraq can become our most powerful asset in the world of public opinion... bar none! As long as we prevail and don't capitulate!

From my educational experience and that perspective, I have always believed that the main crux of the Arab world's hatred of the United States is based on our influence over the world's actions, our dominance of same, and our power within the world, sadly often demonstrated as fear instead. Yet as Kuffars and Infidels to the true believers, our dominance over fundamental Islam is felt as a slap in their God's face!

With Israel more than us, beyond the obvious religious and territorial reasons—we can source their anger towards Israel...to envy.

Of course the Arabs would deny this vehemently and why not. After all, for them it's a bitter pill to swallow this flea on their backs—Israel continues to survive despite their numerous attempts to destroy the state, and it thrives in defiance of their threats and assaults.

Recently, Israel celebrated its sixtieth anniversary of it modern founding. Sixty short years in the scheme of things as they say. Yet in that short chronological amount of time, look at all of the literally amazing accomplishments Israel has achieved against the odds and with such acrimonious neighbors!

Without any major natural resources to depend upon such as oil, this miniscule little country, smaller than the size of New Jersey...is now one of the leading economic powerhouses in the world. A world leader in several high tech industries including IT, bio-medical technology, metals, and software.

Israel's Silicon Wadi (Valley in Hebrew) for example, is ranked number two in importance, only behind California's own Silicon Valley. Israel is also a powerhouse as a free trader and diamond cutter, respected the world over.

So this is truly where the source of this on-going discontent rests at a guttural level. Israel's meteoric rise economically, spews over into hatred and rhetoric within the radical Mosques of the Middle East, fomenting resentment, anger, and hatred outward. Simply said, their neighbors resent and detest Israel's existence for one, and their success secondarily. Perhaps this is where the hatred of the West is truly rooted, who can say for sure. Israel is certainly a glowing example of Western capitalistic success…isn't it?

To those that would argue that the Palestinian issue is at the core of this hatred, I would concede that that argument is put forward to foment by their radical leaders strictly for the benefit of their followers to believe, but the leaders themselves, truly see Israel fundamentally and simply as the ideal target and more likely resent the Israelis for their many successes, and not the more political Palestinian territory issue. According to Taheri, Palestine is strictly mentioned by Naji, in a historical context! How can that be, if the current Palestinian/Israeli conflict is always touted and tied to…and so tantamount to regional peace? In short, even if there were no Palestinian territory issue—there would still be numerous reasons put forward by these radical religious leaders to incite and foment their followers to hatred of the Jewish state. Not to step backward, but Obsession has really said it best, in speaking of how it is always Israel and the Jews fault for every Arab woe: **"What starts with the Jews…never ends with the Jews".** This being the case, I would suggest to Israel's detractors including the UN, that you think twice about always blaming Israel for obstinacy and brutality against the poor, downtrodden, Palestinians who just desire their own state!

I can also suggest that we all remember two other points of significance on this issue. First, remember the Palestinians have in the past, been unwanted and uninvited as refugees within other countries of this region themselves! That's significant in that their fellow occupants of the Middle Eastern region—don't want any of them hanging around within their borders either. Secondly, let's not forget that Israel has demonstrated repeatedly that it is willing to negotiate land for peace with all parties...including with the Palestinians. Just who was it that voluntarily left Palestinian territory behind in the West Bank—anyway?

Nope...simply stated: Israel is the enemy because it's the natural target. Its Western modernity and success stands as a beacon within the region and laughs in the face of failure. These facts create scorn and resentment in the lives of the repressed and deprived of the poor Arab street. It demonstrates to the world that there truly is no excuse for the lack of success and prominence within any country of the Middle East. For if minuscule Israel can create its own prosperity out of nothing, no oil, no natural resources...so too can any other Middle Eastern country. And the fact that there are those Arab countries that have not been as successful on the whole, some even despite their oil exports, it must be Israel's fault somehow, or otherwise it would have to fall on the fault of all of these Arab leaders themselves, and that of course is unfathomable...isn't it?

And before any of Israel's critics jump in with their old, tired claims that Israel is only successful because it has been propped up and unfairly supported for those sixty years by the US like an indulging parent dotes on a child—dream on. Israel's core success is her own.

Yes, the United States has been a great friend and a primary supporter, but that's not to say that Israel isn't a valued ally in a strategic and volatile region of the world. Lastly, the US can't prop up or 'will' any country to succeed, not even itself.

Before closing this chapter, I want to digress for two important paragraphs I'd like you to consider before we move on. They are from Matthew Continetti of the Weekly Standard Magazine. The first paragraph is a repeat from chapter one, yet in its entirety and bears repeating here. The second paragraph concerns the likely Democratic Party nominee as it sums up his purported claim on judgment.

"The left's analysis of Jihadism has been proved incorrect at every turn. It argued military power would be ineffective against the terrorists. Wrong. It argued that intervention in Iraq would energize bin Laden's movement. That movement is in shambles. The left argued Iraq was a lost cause. It isn't. The left argues that a "war on terrorism" is futile, that defeat is inevitable, because terrorism is a "tactic" and not an enemy. Nonsense. President Bush has demonstrated through perseverance and (more often than not) sound policy that the war on terror can be won. And right now…we're winning it."

"Barack Obama has said that the new policy (referring to the surge) would neither "make a dent" in the violence plaguing Iraq nor "change the dynamics" there. A month after the president's announcement, Obama declared it was time to remove American combat troops from Iraq. In April, as the surge brigades were on their way to the combat zone, Senate Democratic leader Harry Reid proclaimed "this war is lost" and that U.S. troops should pack up and come home. In July, as surge operations were underway, the New York Times editorialized that "it is time for the United States to leave Iraq." The Times' editorial writers recognized Iraq "could be even bloodier and more chaotic after Americans leave" but that didn't matter. "Keeping troops in Iraq will only make things worse."—Matthew Continetti 06/02/8, reporting in the Weekly Standard.

Consider for the moment the weighty significance of these two quotes. They offer a prelude, a vision if you will, of where our friends on the left would have likely taken our country already, if given the opportunity. Given what you now know is a worldwide threat to our Western way of life, despite your personal politics, do you honestly think our country will benefit from a radical change in policy on this subject as exercised through our electoral process?

Think about it.

Chapter Seven

What's the status on our key enemies?

Where is this heading?

Now that we've summarized how our military efforts are doing, let's discuss the latest information on what's happening with our enemies in Iraq and elsewhere.

Make no mistake about it, our enemies, both the transnational groups such as Al Qaida, and their state-sponsors, are still focused on their Holy Jihad to ultimately destroy the West and everything we stand for. I quick read of Amir Taheri's article on Naji, clearly bears this fact out.

It can certainly be said that when Taheri titles his article 'Plan B', he is acknowledging Al Qaida's failures in Iraq specifically that followed the successes of 9/11. Precisely, Taheri titled his piece: *"FAILURES PROMPT NEW IDEAS FOR TERROR FROM THE SHADOWS."*

Among Naji's key manifesto recommendations, according to Taheri's article, are these:

"In a notable departure from past al Qaeda strategy, Naji recommends countless small operations that render daily life <u>unbearable</u>, rather than a few spectacular attacks such as 9/11: The 'infidel' leaving his home every morning, should be unsure whether...he'll return in the evening."

Naji's book is entitled as I've previously mentioned... Governance in the Wilderness. All lands outside of Islamic control are the Wilderness, and are not therefore subject to the security of the Jihad, or in simpler terms...are subject to being overthrown!

Naji's argument in his manifesto is that:

"The 'wilderness' will provide the cover for bases for Jihad operations. Jihad would be everywhere, rather than in just one or two countries that the 'infidel' could hit with superior firepower.

Naji further states: "These parallel societies could resemble the 'liberated zones' set up by Marxist guerrillas in parts of Latin America in the last century." –Amir Taheri, July 2, 2008, in the New York Post.

Today, we see these shadowy parallel societies already solidly in place in Western cities such as Paris and London. They infiltrate slowly, methodically, and thoroughly, until they become'overnight' phenomena of sorts and when they become publicly known you can bet your bottom dollar...the damage has already been done!

The riots in Paris were certainly as orchestrated as the bombings in London, they were simply different objectives. How long before we discover there are 'cells' or parallels here in America? Do you remember a few years back, when authorities in Oregon realized that outsiders were trying to set up some type of compound in Bly, Oregon? Ironically, I lived for a short time in Bly in 1970, a town at the time of less than four hundred if I recall correctly! It was a one street

Weyerhaeuser mill town. With ranches so large that they were on the Oregon state map, almost anything could be hidden if you will…perhaps a community of Jihadist cells isn't too far of a stretch!

This new dynamic of transnational Jihadist warfare has many advantages for our enemies. Primarily, it allows state-players of terrorism, to play by proxy for as long as it serves them. Recently we learned that Hezbollah did a lot of the behind the scenes training in Iraq. Naturally this was under the back-story support of Iran.

Don't get me wrong, there will come a point in time in this conflict when the proxy days will end, and the state sponsors will directly enter the ruckus and expose their full agendas… this will commence with phase two of their assault. And one of them we can call—The Mystery State Sponsor of Murder! But first, let's discuss two of our enemies: Syria and Iran.

It became clear to me that Syria was up to something, when they did not attack Israel this last fall, after Israel bombed their new reactor under construction. I of course, had to ask the proverbial question—why didn't they attack? I think I can best predict the answer:

Syria's lack of response and near silence, demonstrates to me that Damascus is not willing to risk a premature chance at attacking Israel and exposing itself. Perhaps they are part of a larger plan; already in place from a united Jihadi front and set to commence the war's second phase, later this year or next!

In Damascus, we find another leading state-sponsor of terrorism, and certainly Iran's cohort in Jihad. A founding member of the State Department's list of state-sponsored terrorism back in 1979 (approaching thirty years now) these bad boys and girls—still remain there…the only remaining original member!

Damascus also appears to get the hospitality award within the state-sponsors of terrorism, by playing host to most of the externally placed leaders of several terror organizations, such as Hamas, among many others! Due to their geographic location within the region, they are a must stop…Ports of Call for every Jihadist and Terrorist leader it seems.

Damascus has also attempted to paint itself as contributing to reducing terror issues as of late; however their sincerity remains questionable, if not dubious. Make no mistake, Syria longs for Israel's destruction even as they negotiate with them behind the scenes for the Golan Heights—perhaps this is yet another ploy of this Jihadi group's larger plan. Are they trying to lull Israel into a false sense of security—only time will tell?

Now as we turn our attention towards Iran, it seems that the only question remaining unanswered at this point is whether Israel bombs Iran's reactors first (as the Jihadists hope they will…forcing Iran to respond…as planned), or might some group or country force an altercation and retaliatory response from Israel first…remember Lebanon in 2006?

For all intents and purposes, the parties politicking for this honor…could include Syria, Hamas in Palestine, Iran, and/or Hezbollah…or any combination there of.

I'm actually coming round to the belief that Israel will likely make the first move again, this time bombing Iran's reactors. As they have done before against Saddam's Iraq back in the eighties, and what they did to Syria this past year—Israel only stands silent for so long…then takes decisive action.

Another point to consider is that the timing is critical. A Hamas spokesman already expressed his desire to see Obama elected—and what does that tell you? With the American elections coming up and an unknown future administration looming with questionable loyalties, I believe the Israelis sought and received an implicit okay from their proven ally— President Bush in Washington, when the two countries met last week—and of course—only time will tell. Hell…it may have already happened! Remember there was a nine month black out on the Syrian bombings, although in the case of Iran, I seriously doubt it will be kept quiet.

According to Taheri's article, Naji states in his new book…that:

"*The only Western power still capable of resisting is the United States, he believes. But that, too, will change once President Bush is gone."—Amir Taheri, July 2, 2008—New York Post.*"

I am of the opinion that President Bush can take the above quote as the greatest honor he could receive—your enemy admitting you made a singular difference in the war's outcome to date. Our naysaying friends should take note of this…historians certainly will.

Naturally if any conflict comes to pass, expect oil prices to climb to +/- $200. per barrel overnight, **as long as we remain beholden to OPEC Oil—that is.** Beyond oil—could World War III centered on this global jihad…be far behind?

The Israelis realize, that having neighbors with nuclear missiles—pointing at them…is counterproductive to their survival…and certainly a peaceful Sabbath.

And for their part, the Islamic Republic's government in Tehran has gone out of its way through Mr. Charisma himself…Ahmadinejad, to continually goad Israel incessantly about their impending destruction…doesn't he? Honestly, some times I have to wonder what Ahmadinejad is thinking. If he kills off all the Israelis, there go their brilliant doctors along with everyone else. As such Mahmoud, who in hell will you get to do your nose job? I mean—really?

Ahmadinejad's threats speak of a tyrant who wants this to be a conflict with Israel of self-fulfilled destiny and biblical proportions. I believe he plans to wait out their first strike attack, so that he may destroy them not only completely, but zealously and passionately as well or at least attempt to with lots of help!

Naturally I have to hope that Tel Aviv realizes the scope and power of the forces they are pinned against and have planned accordingly. I have no doubt you see, that Tehran has a few surprises in store for Israel's attack—such as perhaps a biological element or maybe even an old untraceable errant nuclear warhead from the former Soviets!

Yet for Ahmadinejad, every day brings a new opportunity to threaten and rant. *"I tell you that with the unity and awareness of all the Islamic countries—all of the satanic powers will be destroyed,"—Mahmoud Ahmadinejad. To a group of foreign visitors ahead of the 19th anniversary of the death of revolutionary leader Ayatollah Ruhollah Khomeini. As reported on Fox News Online 06/ 02/08*

Iran is the most active player so far, of the few exposed state sponsors of this Jihad. Their Islamic Revolutionary Guard Corps and their Ministry of Intelligence and Security are their chief terrorist components. Along with their involvement and proxy activities in Iraq, they have close involvement with Palestinian terror groups and the Lebanese Hezbollah. Iran is a major enabler of anti-Israel terror, threats to Saudi Arabia's monarchy…and supplies training, money, and safe-haven to various Shiite terrorist sects and groups.

Ahmadinejad has at least been very consistent in his anti-Western rhetoric and verbal thrashing attacks on Israel and the US. *"Today, the time for the fall of the satanic power of the United States has come and the countdown to the annihilation of the emperor of power and wealth has started."—Mahmoud Ahmadinejad. Reported by Fox News Online on 06/02/08*

And not that I want to be taken as insincere…or insensitive…but were a President Obama let's say, to fly over and break bread with Mahmoud…what does he possibly call the guy, you know, sort of…as a nickname…to break the ice? Really I suppose, it's either 'Mock', 'Muddy' …or otherwise…Moody? I would suggest 'Dinny' but that might be construed as a little 'too-light-in-the-loafer' for old Moody and homophobic Iran, isn't it? Anyway you slice it, it isn't exactly easy bringing this guy home to meet your folks, is it?

Yet, I think we can all agree that that fantastic Obama wit—providing his teleprompter's hooked up, will win old Moody over…won't it

Lastly, Iran's on-going standoff with the UN over nuclear ambitions, is well known, documented, and is another focal point in this Global conflict.

Iran represents many diverse elements of this Jihad under one catch-all roof. Tehran's government as a theologically abducted fanatical regime has been a principle state player and directly involved within proxy activities of support for the Iraq insurgent forces. Their Ayatollahs and other clerics are among the most outspoken on Iranian TV and elsewhere of anti-Western rhetoric, as you'll see when you watch Obsession. The country's fundamental Islamic beliefs have already been shown to be among the most radical and intolerant within the region, especially towards Saudi Arabia and of course Israel. They are the primary exposed force within the worldwide conflict as I see it!

Chapter Eight

Our Mystery State Sponsor of Murder.

A New Enemy...requires a change of strategy.

Now at the risk of alienating anyone reading this narrative, I can't possibly conclude this book without mentioning the guiltiest of these Middle-Eastern countries. Guilty at least as it relates to creating the foundation and roots for this radical Islamic Jihad and the murder it preaches. Of course I'm speaking of our mystery sponsor and here they are, that royally corrupt, two-faced, oil-manipulating—kingdom of deceit and thievery, Saudi Arabia...come on down!

Our relationship with the Saudis was at one time a worthwhile, win/win relationship... at least it started out that way. We wanted stability and a strategic ally in the region.

Remember, Israel wasn't founded until 1948 and we're talking about right as WWII was ending. We saw Saudi Arabia's control of the Arabian Peninsula and its enormous oil reserves as very appealing. Ironically, it was surveying by our own US Oil companies that discovered the greater percentage of those reserves.

The Saudis offered us a guarantee of a stable oil 'partner' who likewise also guaranteed us a fair and moderate price for that oil. And with the Cold War's commencement only months away, the Saudi partnership put us into a strategic relationship for unlimited oil to go head to head against the oil-rich Soviets.

Based upon the above advantages, our own self-serving government made an agreement with the house of Saud—their royal family. They pledged to protect the Saudi Monarchy and defend the country against all comers with a large contingent of US troops placed within the kingdom.

Laurent Murawiec joined the Rand Corporation as a senior policy analyst in 1999. Educated at the Sorbonne and having served the French government within their Ministry of Defense, Murawiec is a US/Saudi expert. Here's what he has to say about this relationship.

... *"The original reasons for this marriage of convenience have long since faded away...It is time for a divorce!" Laurent Murawiec briefing of November 19, 2002 as reported in the Middle East Forum.*

Murawiec also points out: *"To counter the proliferation of anti-Saudi, Iranian propaganda however, the Saudis decided to go along with funding the spread of radical Wahhabi Islam teachings abroad. The royal family's oil wealth poured into countries throughout the Islamic world, from West Africa to Indonesia, fueling a proliferation of Madrassas (religious schools) that indoctrinated a new generation of radical Islamists. Even in the United States, Muslim children have studied Islamic 'primers' shipped from Wahhabi institutes in Saudi Arabia"—Laurent Murawiec briefing of November 19, 2002 as reported in the Middle East Forum.*

Using their oil as leverage, they have managed to manipulate our government into being their own personal security forces, **while they take a fair amount of the oil profits they earn from us, and hand it right over to the very people trying to destroy us...these radical Wahhabi Islamic elements within their kingdom.** This tithe so-as-to-speak, **keeps these Wahhabi radicals within their country appeased, and from otherwise over-throwing this corrupt monarchy**...only for the time being, in my opinion. Remember what I warned about appeasing these radicals?

One would think that an ally that enjoys and benefits from the kind of support the US government has provided for decades dating back to FDR, the Saud family would hold their relationship with America preciously and in high esteem, regard, and respect. Well, here's a short quote from their late King Fahd—that I think perfectly illustrates the kingdom's very loyal feelings towards us...best:

"I summon my blue-eyed slaves anytime it pleases me. I command the Americans to send me their bravest soldiers to die for me. Anytime I clap my hands, a stupid genie called the American ambassador appears to do my bidding. Whenever the Americans die in my service, their bodies are frozen in metal boxes by the US Embassy and American airplanes carry them away, as if they never existed. Truly, America is my favorite slave."

King Fahd Bin Abdul-Aziz, Jeddah, 1993 Quoted from sauduction@sauduction.com

And what will the radical Wahhabi Islamic elements within the kingdom continue to do with all our US/Saudi charity cash at these record prices...you ask? Beyond a mere network of radical Madrassas—these shadowy centers of radical worship will allow the Holy Jihad's tentacles to stretch around the world, and to infiltrate the many wildernesses, as laid out in Taheri's article on Naji's Plan B. They will use this network to fund localized terrorist operations around the entire globe…most notably—under the scattered banner of Al Qaida! Their goal is simple:

"The Islamic movement must be global - fighting everywhere, all the time, and on all fronts."—Amir Taheri July 2, 2008, in the New York Post.

If we allow this asinine **revenue stream of hate** to continue, then these charities will continue to fund terrorist activities and groups around the globe. Terrorist attacks that are specifically focused on destroying the United States and all of its friends and allies—as evidenced by this Holy Jihad!

Sadly we don't have to be the sharpest knives in the drawer to ask the obvious question: **What kind of lunacy are we allowing our government to perpetuate here?**

All of this charity funding naturally, becomes possible… only from the sale of that wonderful Saudi Oil. The oil you and I must depend upon, because our Congress has placed their own special-interest agenda over the well-being and independence of their fellow Americans for years. Their agenda dates back to at least 1982 when they legislated to curtail all offshore drilling, as well as exploration in ANWR. Well friends…this must no longer be tolerated by anyone in either political party, and I mean that sincerely.

Today in our current Congress, there are many members apparently beholden to the environmental special interests… and they have successfully over the years, done the bidding for these groups. They have simply regulated the US oil companies up to their corporate 'necks' in order to minimize any drilling domestically for more of our own oil which we have an abundant supply of. They don't care about you and me; they don't even really care if gas costs five bucks a gallon. These members don't want to drill for one stinking barrel of oil and perpetuate fossil fuel consumption one day longer than necessary...case frigging closed!

And if I hear even one more dang member of Congress say that we can't fix this energy crisis by drilling—and that it will do us no good...I'm going to scream! What about domestic drilling's ability to make it possible to stop sending billions of dollars into the hands of the G_d Damn terrorists trying to murder us? That won't help to fix the crisis? What about that? What's the excuse now? Oh I know...let me guess...it will cost too much...or it will take too long...so let's just do absolutely nothing while these bastards kill our fellow Americans!

True, some of our known oil reserves would be a tad pricier to reclaim than other foreign options. And yet some of it, like that in ANWR (the Arctic National Wildlife Refuge), is expected to have huge potential and have a far more productive volume than current lands the oil industry is allowed to drill on. Here's what the US Energy Information Agency has to say about the potential in ANWR:

"The opening of ANWR to oil and gas development includes the following impacts: reducing world oil prices, reducing the U.S. dependence on imported foreign oil, improving the U.S. balance of trade, extending the life of TAPS (the Alaskan Pipeline) for oil, and increasing U.S. jobs."—United States 2007 Annual Energy Review, 2008.

The 2008 United States Geologic Survey just released, contends that there are ninety billion barrels of discoverable oil and natural gas waiting for us in the Arctic!

Any way you slice it, there is plenty of oil for the taking in the good old US of A...all we have to do is expand our exploration and drilling for it! I don't know about you, but this pisses me off something royal, pardon the pun! And there's so much more to the Saudis' tomfoolery.

Vali Nasr is an associate professor of political science at the University of San Diego. He is an expert on Islamic extremism.   Here's what he had to say on the Saudi role in terrorism, as relayed in an interview with PBS's Frontline:

"In fact, this whole phenomenon that we are confronting, (terrorism) which Al Qaeda is a part of, is very closely associated with Saudi Arabia's financial and religious projects for the Muslim world as a whole.   All of these (terrorist) groups are rooted in a network of seminaries, or as the term is called in the local vernacular, "Madrassa".   My argument was that the main source of funding for these groups is Saudi Arabia."

Frontline: "So you're saying that Saudi Arabia is funding the milieu, if you will, the atmosphere, from which this Islamic extremism has emerged?"

"That's correct, Saudi Arabia has been the single biggest source of funding for fanatical interpretations of Islam, and the embodiment of that interpretation is organizations and schools has created a self-perpetuating institutional basis for promoting fanaticism across the Muslim world...There is no other state who spends as much money at ensuring conservatism and fanaticism among Muslims.   The result is "the increasing entrenchment of rigidity and fanaticism in the Muslim world".—Vali Nasr, 10/25/01 Interview in PBS's Frontline

I share the belief as a political scientist and behaviorist, that this rigidity and fanaticism as preached in the Mosques, then taught in the Madrassas, is the root cause for this global jihad—this Holy War, and I honestly don't believe the whole movement would have even been possible...without these foundation-building Saudi charity investments!   And it's all possible and coming from...our damn oil money!

How does this make you feel?   To know in reality that this worldwide battle we are involved with now, was at its roots created as a diversionary tactic put forward by one Royal family to protect its kingdom?   It all originates with a fear of being overthrown by its own radical elements.   So

now the rest of the free world is at risk as a result…and you and I are paying the tab every frigging time we fill up!

Worst of all as I've demonstrated, but it bears repeating how these members of Congress can have the gall to say that our own drilling will not help? When doing so, will get us the hell off of Saudi oil that finances…our own purposed extinction!

Look guys and gals, there's plenty of fault to go around, so let's look at the President for a minute too. I won't blame President Bush for this Holy War. Analyzing what we know now, I feel he at least has taken many effective steps to answer the call of these Islamo Fascists. This enemy who wishes to Islamosize us as they themselves have now admitted—must be stopped, let's be honest. Yet no one's perfect and I will fault him personally for the following:

President Bush from my perspective has failed us and by extension his own so-called War on Terror, by being disingenuous over the role of Saudi Arabia for the last six and a half years! He has known since the initial post-attack intelligence was delivered to his desk no doubt, that the Saudis are no friend to this country…or his administration…or any administration for that matter. Clearly the knowledge of the Saud family's complacency in all of this terror alone is enough for anyone to take a more aggressive approach with these enablers a long time ago. Yet now with $135 per barrel oil we don't even need to think about it really…do we?

We can all recall President Bush's powerful speech before a joint session of the United States Congress after 9/11 **when he promised that we would bring those responsible to bear for the losses of 9/11. He also cited that one tool he would use to stop these terrorists, was to cut off their financial assets and sources of funding—remember that?**

Well, did he do anything to impact Saudi Arabia's financial influence with this revenue stream to these terrorist groups through those charities? Hardly.

Naturally, the President did have some strong motivations not to push the Saudis—then…but now is a different day with $135 a barrel oil. But was Bush's approach the right decision in hindsight? I really don't think so, but let's review the possible reasons he had to consider:

Such a move would be viewed negatively in several circles, not the least of which would be on the Arab Street (who already distrusted us for decades), our Allies (as it would force them to take sides), and from some members within our own Congress (that from the onset, had questionable faith in Bush's judgment…a painful election result—still fresh in their minds).

Not wanting to increase the size and scope of the new conflict, by naming an old, albeit questionable—ally, as one of the axis of terror. This one move to be sure, would end a 50 plus year relationship of at least some strategic importance. Not to mention all of our troops placed on Saudi soil that might be needed—another important consideration complicating the decision dynamics.

Trying to avoid further problems and hardships as the result of any interruption in the supply of oil when we were simultaneously preparing our country and military for an extended and protracted war with a completely new type of enemy.

Never one to be accused for being too bright for his own good—to put it politely, but one of the many subjects the president understands critically well—is oil. It is after all, his family's business for decades and his family has enjoyed a long personal relationship with the Saud dynasty coincidentally. I am not insinuating anything more than stating this known fact…the two families are friends.

I honestly believe the President had legitimate concerns on risking cutting off a large supplier of oil, and this is demonstrable by looking at how he is currently protecting the strategic oil reserve, as if it were his first-born child!

The sincere hope that diplomacy with the Saudis could be far more productive than calling them out for their complacency with Al Qaida. In other words, the belief, that they were a more important, strategic and effective ally—than dangerous as an enemy.

From the beginning, the president seemed to be more than willing to ignore the Saudis' indirect involvement with the War on Terror, as they were in the back-story if you will, and at least initially, I do not believe their complicity truly was recognized as so substantial.

You know, for all of the 'right' decisions the President made at the beginning of this war, his Saudi policy—certainly wasn't one of them…regrettably! We have lost valuable time in our Holy War, and our enemy is now more formidable and enriched, because of the president's avoidance of not calling the Saudis out early on.

I don't want to belabor this, but the Saudis know exactly what they're doing…and they callously make it look easy. We've heard their late King's comments and the bile is still lying in the back of my throat, thinking of those vicious words again.

The bottom line here, is that our brave heroes within all branches of the service deserve much better, and at a guttural level—they have been insulted and abused to be called the King's—blue-eyed slaves.

As someone who has studied and gained an understanding of this crazy subject known as…political science, I acknowledge that it could prove challenging to defend the administration's decision on keeping their mouths—shut on the Saudi issue.

It's clear that President Bush realizes more than most, just how guilty the Saudis are. Further, having all of that oil background himself, he is keenly aware of how the Saudis had already sold the US down the river decades ago in the 70's. Yes—they went against their agreement with us to help create OPEC as an oil producers cartel. And naturally, no other producer benefited more from the creation of this body, then they...themselves.

As I said when I began this section on Saudi Arabia, the House of Saud are masterful manipulators indeed.

Today, more than at any other time in our history, and for more fundamentally important and crucial reasons to our National Security, this idiotic Saudi policy must not continue for one day longer than necessary!

In Riyadh, Saudi Arabia, the Royal Family by some estimates **gives around 20-25% of their massive annual income generated from oil sales, to their charities. As stated, these are hardly traditional charities; they are under the auspices and control of radical Wahhabi Islam fundamentalist leaders within Saudi Arabia. These leaders then distribute it outward to their Madrassas, where it is eventually fanned out to all of their terrorist organizations around the globe.**

These groups then turn their attentions on bringing Jihad and terror destruction to us and our friends and allies...and count on 'Plan B' as Taheri's article has said, to be a far more localized and simple affair to keep greater numbers of us in utter fear.

"Naji recommends kidnappings, the holding of hostages, the use of women and children as human shields, exhibition killings to terrorize the enemy, suicide bombings and countless gestures that make normal life impossible for the "infidel" and Muslim collaborators. The West has no stomach for a long fight. Once our parallel societies are established throughout the world, they would exert pressure on non-Muslims to submit. Naji believes that, subjected to constant intimidation and fear of death, most non-Muslims (especially in the West) would submit"—Amir Taheri, July 2, 2008, in the New York Post.

Beyond the terror itself, it seems to me, that these Jihadists are still focused on destroying the West—financially. Don't forget, these idiots believed that they could bring down our entire financial system if they could successfully bring down the symbolic World Trade Center towers...why do you think they didn't give up after 1993? More than anything else, these Jihadists want our supposed strength (capitalist wealth) to be the cause and harbinger of our own demise. This defeat would then be sermonized as just punishment for going against the fundamental teachings of Allah.

Being that financial disaster didn't occur as they had hoped, planned, and predicted when the towers went down, isn't it just possible that all of this current OPEC oil manipulation,—is simply another effort of their earlier threat? Do these Jihadists and their state sponsors (Saudi Arabia among them!) believe $200 a barrel oil will succeed where 757-improvized explosives failed? Perhaps we will not know the true answer to this question for some time.

So far, when oil eclipsed a 'mere' $135 per barrel, we already had a horribly weak dollar, and the economy—while not in a recession as of this date, certainly is on shaky ground. Wall Street is in questionable shape loaded with uncertainty and headed for a bear market. With $4. + a gallon gas and $5. Diesel fuel cost, and a dangerous sign of Carter-era inflation looming in our near future...Wall Street is pensive...as the Jihadists...hope!

And the people who benefit from all of these US dollars paying for high oil...take our money and recycle it straight to their Jihadist warriors—who continue to try to kill all of us dead!

Many would argue that the Information Revolution is a powerful ally. No time in our history since fighting the British for our independence—have we citizens had more direct and accessible power to persuade our government. Thanks to the power of the internet and the blogs, and American Citizens protectionist organizations like American Solutions and/or

GrassFire. Org borne out of the internet age—we can again, become a powerful force to be reckoned with.

We can wield great changes within our own country… and within the world as a result…and we have little time to spare. You see, our enemies are already using the Internet to advance their cause and to recruit, educate, and train their Fascist converts! So we must use it as well to unite our side and to bring pressure to bear continuously on our leaders, until the bastards either start doing their jobs as is their duty or we throw out the lot of them…its enough!

One thing is certain, our National Security interests—demand immediate steps be taken—so let's start with these a-holes in Congress.

Our message to our Congress must be clear, unveiled, and concise: We will either bring all dissenting members of Congress to embrace—energy policy…enlightenment—or…their retirement! They either join with us and protect us with comprehensive reform that includes domestic drilling legislation to get us through this crisis, or they'll be clearing out one office after another—at their next reelection cycle. Perhaps these unemployed former members of Congress can find new careers monitoring the mating habits of the Caribou, who by the way enjoy the warmth created by the Alaskan Pipeline as they're breeding! I might point out that we may have never found out about this phenomenon if it hadn't been for all the cigarette butts found alongside the pipeline!

In all seriousness, I don't know about you, but I have personally found many recent comments by some members of our Congress, outright insulting. How dare them! They sit there and threaten and/or chastise the Oil companies for their outrageous profits or salaries…when the US Congress has **passed laws taking twice the amount in tax dollars from the sale of a gallon of gas, as the oil companies themselves earn in net profits, in return for all of their investments within their businesses.** And have you heard yet…they want to raise that tax...right now with $4. a gallon for gas...what are they smoking up there on that hill?

Understand something...the obstinacy we've recently seen out of this Congress, specifically some of its passionate Democratic members over domestic drilling is no accident! This is likely going to take a major amount of pressure to get them to capitulate believe me. If you don't believe me, just watch. They will create every excuse in the book why we can't drill...and every stupid alternative solution we don't need!

These Democrats are so absolutely against *any* newly expanded drilling for a single barrel of oil anywhere within the geographic contents of this country or its waters...because they are wholly beholden to the environmentalists for their donations and jobs...**so screw you and me!** And see, the greenies want to get us off the Texas Tea, and so they demonize any attempt to explore and drill, thereby forcing us into this corner known as foreign oil...**well no more...they don't call it Texas Tea for nothing!**

The environmentalists goal has always been eliminating fossil fuel consumption altogether. In the long run, most of their reasons are sound, prudent, and important...and dare I say...admirable! Yet first it must be shown that these goals are obtainable, sustainable,—and available in the here and now, and that includes while protecting our National Security interests concurrently!

Our green friends want us all driving hybrids and electrics tomorrow, but that's just not practical today, sorry guys but it's not. Timing is everything.

Think I'm wrong—well think again. Let's assume that tomorrow morning at 9:01 a.m. a Lithium battery researcher stumbles onto the last holdup for a renewable, long-term, sustainable, and powerful battery, viable enough for all automotive use, including tractor-trailer trucks.

A plug-in electric car can finally be produced that can go 300 miles on a single charge, while a larger battery, could power commercial trucks four times that distance on a single charge—our problems are solved…right?   **Wrong!** Where do you expect to get enough electricity to 'charge' all of these millions of batteries?

We don't currently manufacture anywhere near that amount of electricity, and our national power grid is antiquated at best. And here again…the environmentalists will say…oh no, no—don't even think of suggesting we use clean coal technology to generate that electricity! So you see, it's not as easy as it looks, is it?

Perhaps we only need to remind Congress of a key point here. **They serve—you and I, and not the other way around** and they must set priorities and develop solutions— not rhetoric, that is based on the greatest needs of the country at any given moment, and not pushing their own pet special interests groups as it suits them, ahead of our most-pressing national security concerns.

And in the final analysis, ask yourself, what good is a pristine, 100% protected environment matter…if our enemies have killed all of us off…and our culture is wiped off of the planet? When is the earth worth so much—that no one fights to save an entire culture—inhabiting it? Let's get real here folks.

I believe that we can be good stewards of the earth's best interests, while still providing for our own human inhabitants too. We'll discuss this in greater depth a little later, but for now, here are those steps we can take to develop some real solutions to this crisis:

To begin with, we call for Congress to enact new legislation immediately to begin regulating the commodities markets, specifically aimed at oil speculation. We need to get this market segment back to where it was before miniscule margin calls made it such a boon for opportunist investors.

According to political consultant Dick Morris, the number of investment dollars within this market has grown twenty fold as an investment vehicle, and that ought to tell you something right there. As always, Dick Morris.com is an excellent source of information on a variety of political subjects, his commentary on the Oil Speculators is no exception.

We must also ask President Bush to make some immediate policy changes prior to his leaving office. Some of these he will embrace enthusiastically, while others will take our maximum resolve to influence him—in short, we need to call him out on his own mistakes as it concerns the Saudis. Let's assume we convince him.

I believe that all of these actions can be legally taken by the President's Executive Order privilege under National Security and economic emergency circumstances, at least in the short term. The President can call upon Congress to fill in any gaps for the long term with legislation after the first six-month elimination period.

So we begin unflinchingly as the President announces our policy change in three components:

The first component is the Strategic Oil Supply. The President announces that up to three hundred million barrels of oil will be sold to our refineries at its original purchase price. Two, the President announces a comprehensive yet temporary energy-rationing program. The final component announces the bold move to immediately cease and stop—100% of all oil imports from any OPEC country but Iraq—no exceptions, in the name of our National Security. Let them all burn in hell with their lovely oil…to fuel the fire as they say!

Next, we need to call home our Ambassador to Saudi Arabia immediately without warning, and symbolically send their Ambassador packing, as well. We inform the Saud family that their intolerable actions have finally caused our government to rethink our one-sided, long-term strategic relationship with them and OPEC, and that has led us onto a new path: **America's freedom from—OPEC dependence!** Believe me, by this point in time…we will have gotten Saudi

Arabia's attention and they will be making all kinds of offers to us (in strict secrecy) and let them, they're talking to the hand.

Personally speaking, I don't feel we need to say or justify anything any further than this. The Saudis have known for years that they have been pushing the U.S. further away and siding against us, particularly since the creation of OPEC, and that surely one day…they would push the envelope a barrel too far. Well, that day is here…hooray!

Now here are the statistics we must review and resolve:

Our current oil consumption is +/-20,500,000 barrels a day and falling, with an additional consumption of 64 million gallons of refined gasoline being imported each day—quite an appetite, ha? Since we have expanded refineries coming on line as early as 2010, I'm going to leave this part of our shortfall as it is, as it will work itself out.

As a nation with mostly mature wells, we are down to pumping a mere 9 barrels of oil a day, per well with +/- 510,000 wells total. Domestically speaking, we are only capable right now of fulfilling 40% of our domestic oil needs. By comparison, Russian wells nearly double our current production today, when only a few years back, their production nearly mirrored ours. While our Democratic friends in Congress consistently stopped us from increasing our drilling and pumping capacity (the voting records don't lie friends)—the Russians didn't have those problems.

And by the way, I need to deviate a little here. You see, our Democratic members of Congress now seem to be touting the fact that the oil industry hasn't drilled sufficiently yet, on any of some sixty eight (68) million acres of leased federal lands they've optioned. As I've already mentioned, some members of Congress will stop at nothing to avoid capitulation on this heartstring of an issue to their collective purse string, if you will. So these oil 'know-it-all's' in Congress, keep threatening to take away the leases from the oil companies (remember their "use it or lose it" rhetoric?).

I'm reminded often of the brilliance of our current 110th Congress, and its House leader, the very powerful…Ms.—**_I'm Nance…and I wear the pants_**—Pelosi. First off, remember, this is the same Congress that enjoys a record low approval rating from the American people of 9%, and their dazzling leader, who most recently took it upon herself to insult our only true ally in Latin America—Columbia. It seems that Madame Speaker has personally held up for a floor vote, their free trade treaty with us, because that government might be unfairly persecuting the rights of the international Marxist terrorist organization—known as FARC. The same government who in the very same week, orchestrated an incredible raid on a secret FARC compound and freed several captives of many years imprisonment, including three Americans! Yes Madam Speaker, you are so brilliant, your judgment is right up there with your colleague from across the hill in the Senate, Barry— I got it right on Iraq—Obama!

So given the stellar leadership of our Congress and their incredible 9% approval rating, of course I felt compelled to do a little snooping around to see what the oil industry was actually doing in 2007 to drill for oil and increase domestic oil supplies, if at all. Since these know-it-alls in Congress purport they've been doing nothing, I figured that should be verifiable. And honestly, I did find out a few things that shocked me, so I must share them with you too, in all candor.

I truly believe most of us realize there are numerous complexities of the oil business that the oil industry faces on an on-going basis. They must satisfy the Federal Government, the EPA and other Federal agencies, assorted State governments, regulators, OSHA, and I could go on and on a while longer but I think you get my point. It's a daunting job and no picnic! In short, nothing happens easily, quickly, or casually. Time and recourses are limited and there are countless hurdles to successfully bridge on so many levels just to drill a single oil well…okay, enough said.

For those naysayers who are already saying "I told you so" right now, assuming the worst and that I'm merely prefacing all of the above because the oil industry's exploration and drilling during 2007 was so abysmal and pathetic, yes read on for the startling statistics.

During the year 2007, our oil companies were in fact… busy! Yes, I said busy, in fact 26% more! Now I don't know about the specifics of our Congress' information, but I have to laugh at these self-confessed mavens of the oil business. You see, our oil industry despite all the hoops they have to jump through…explored and **drilled nearly 50,000 new wells for petroleum products last year in 2007!** Here's the exact breakdown for any 'number fanatics' out there, courtesy of *the 2007 United States D.O.E.—Energy Information Administration's Annual Energy Review. (Since your author felt that was a slightly more reliable source than pulling the information out of his…ass, like apparently Congress has!)*

Our oil industry companies successfully explored and drilled 13,843 new crude oil wells, and 31,252 new natural gas wells—just in 2007. There were an additional 4,052 unsuccessful drills, for a combined 49,147-drilled well sites. And by the way, that means that our oil industry had an exploration and drilling success rate of almost 92% (91.8% to be exact thanks to prescreening those 68 million acres!) and that's some good science and technology isn't it?

I mean, come on, what the hell more can we ask or expect from this industry, for crying out loud? I don't know about you, but right now, I want to personally say something to all of those members of Congress who may be reading this narrative too—and you know who you are. Let me put it this way: It's better to keep one's mouth closed—and appear stupid, then to open it…and eliminate…everyone's doubt! *Author Unknown.*

Now that I got that off my chest, let's go back to our previous subject before I went off point.

Our two largest suppliers of imported oil are fortunately good friends and close allies, Canada and Mexico. Together they account for +/-33% of the 60% of imported oil we consume daily…God bless them, that's over 50% of what we import. This brings us to an adjusted coverage of 73% of our current daily consumption. We get yet another +/-11% of the 60% from other friendly non-OPEC producers such as Great Britain, Norway, Brazil, etc. Lastly, we export a minimal amount of oil ourselves, approximately 1%, therefore if we cease those exports, we can rebuild our coverage to +/-85% of our current consumption daily. Not bad, but it's obviously not enough.

Since this crisis began and with no help from our elected representatives in Congress whatsoever, Americans have bravely and voluntarily gone out of their own way, to begin lowering their thirst for gasoline—and I salute their efforts and we need more. Already these efforts are paying off and making a difference and amount to a +/- drop of over 2% which translates to 150 million barrels conserved over a year's time! So we can add that number of 2% effectively into our adjusted coverage (above) of 85% and it becomes 87% coverage of our daily consumption!

But now its time to ask the real hard questions over this crisis, to wit:

How can we possibly not do something to stop our hard-earned dollars from being swallowed literally by our vehicles—**and turned into terrorist cash for our enemies to use to destroy us?**

How much more can we afford to pay for a gallon of gas, when the current price is already forcing families into financial crisis…and there's no end in sight to the escalating prices?

So its time to talk about **energy rationing** as previously mentioned and I beg you to keep your cool and not overreact and dismiss it, until you hear me out entirely—fair enough?

I know what you're thinking—but consider this solution based on the facts, not emotions.

First, many of us will recall we had rationing for a short time during the gas crisis of the last century, and our greatest generation will recall it during WWII too (and aren't we in a war now too?) It wasn't totally painless, but mostly so, and besides, no one went without. As I recall, we preferred it to our 55 mile-per-hour national speed limit by far. We all adjusted reasonably well to the odd and even system, it was fair, it worked—and it ended those long lines at the pump.

When announced among our three components, we should be able to blow out those high gas prices—nearly overnight—and return 'sanity' to the world market for oil which affects all Americans directly and here's how.

Our 2007 net oil imports amounted to approximately 12,040,000 barrels of oil a day! The world's estimated total oil production per day in 2007 was 73.27 million barrels for all OPEC and Non-OPEC producers. This means the United States itself, consumed **27% of the entire world's oil production per day during 2007**—that's some 'demand' distinctly on its own!

OPEC alone represented production of 32.18 million barrels a day for 2007! Of that figure, we imported approximately 5,357,800 barrels of oil from OPEC countries in 2007 (therefore approximately 16.67% of OPEC's oil ends up in US-bound tankers...so we are importing 44.5% of our 60% of oil imports—directly from OPEC! Our imports in 2007 from Saudi Arabia alone were 1,489,000 barrels a day, which means that nearly 28% of our OPEC imports are coming from Saudi Arabia's production daily! *United States D.O.E.—Energy Information Administration's Annual Energy Review-2007.*

Now to conclude these statistics; please allow me unemotionally to give you one more…that will likely disgust you! According to numerous sources as previously stated, 20-25% of all of Saudi Arabia's oil money ends up into the hands of these radical Wahhabi Jihadists and their terror organizations and Madrassas.

If current levels and prices of imported oil from the Saudis are maintained through 2008, by year's end that will equal +/- 543,485,000 barrels of oil! Assuming $135. per barrel were to end up as an annualized averaged cost per barrel, (it's likely to be lower, honestly) that would equate to: $73,370,475,000.! Hell, let's just round it down to a mere seventy three (73) billion dollars, chump change! And that's what we would be—chumps! Because after their exorbitant production costs of about $2-3 bucks a barrel…Allah forbid, the Saudi family will enjoy a modest net profit of: $71,740,030,000.! Much of that is spent greasing the palms of the Royal Family and passes through that 71 billion into all kinds of directions. Some is invested in trying to buy as much of American real estate and other interests, along with US Treasury Bills.

Now get ready to be disgusted: That means at 20% donated to their terrorist charities, they will fund $14,348,006,000 directly to terrorist interests in 2008 that seek the annihilation of the United States of America. You and me, all of our children, parents, family, and friends… our American way of life! And naturally, if they give more, say 25% to these wonderful charities, the number goes up to nearly eighteen (18) billion dollars!

Well, have I convinced you yet? How do you feel, knowing that **we're sending $14 billion of our oil dollars over to Saudi Arabia's most radical elements and Jihadi terrorists to destroy us?** Does this justify gas rationing to you? You bet-your-ass, as they beautifully say on the streets of Brooklyn!

We must decapitate this Jihadi movement one way or the other...our future depends upon it. And it's interesting, but both sides of this conflict...must go after the finances of the other side, to have a chance of accomplishing their respective goals.

But like we've discussed if we announce our freedom from—OPEC dependence tomorrow...we'd see gas at the pump drop dramatically within days! Don't believe me, look at it logically.

We as one consuming country represent 27% of the earth's oil consumption daily as I've detailed, and our imports alone represent 16%. If we were to stop importing OPEC oil (only) of approximately 5.357 million barrels per day which represents nearly 7.5% of the world's daily production, that surplus would at least initially greatly reverse the direction of oil prices...and likely dramatically so.

How low will it drop...I'm not an expert in this field, so I don't rightly know...nor do I want to *speculate* emotionally like the commodities markets...pardon the pun. I'd prefer to guess personally, so I suggest we call in the experts to answer this query. What I do know, is that this whole supply/demand vs. speculator interpretation, has driven year-to-date, all time high values for a barrel of oil based on its future value...due to predicting extremely tight supplies on a daily basis.

Oil futures, short supply, and a weak dollar, are all driving these record prices. So why not kick those prices in the ass for all the crap they've put us through these last several months? Will I personally be sorry for these speculators if their futures go $80 short—per barrel overnight, or if the Saudi family has to live with $60. per barrel...I don't think so!

It seems to me that oil should have a real dollar value without all this mumbo jumbo, close to 2006's ending prices anyway, if you consider the impact of freeing up 7.5% of the world's production overnight...simply put. Imagine the impact on prices and futures if OPEC were to announce tomorrow that they were increasing oil production five million barrels per day. That's the magnitude of this policy change in effect. So despite what our Congress' Democratic leadership might try to argue, freeing up supply does translate to lower prices...case closed.

When averaged by the individual costs per barrel of the entire world's oil producers...OPEC and Non-OPEC, the price of a barrel of light sweet crude was just under $60. per barrel. I believe that figure is a fair place to start the guessing for where a barrel of oil might 'land' after our bold pronouncement.

The retail cost basis for a gallon of gas therefore, should equate to a retail price at the pump of +/-, $1.89 per gallon on the low side for regular unleaded gasoline, up to around $2.25 on the high side, with diesel number two coming in well under $2.50 per gallon...offering a return to sanity, and freeing us from any possible Jihadist-inspired Middle-East efforts to bankrupt us.

Naturally these estimates are based on lower costs for the imported oil from all friendly exporters, which should be another consequence of falling oil prices from us pulling out of the OPEC buyer's market. And truly speaking, we help the entire world in this crisis, don't we? I believe by our sacrifice, we show the world what Americans are made of and perhaps we regain some of the respect we've supposedly lost since 9/11 and Iraq.

I suspect that OPEC may initially rebel and freeze large production percentages across the board and who cares! Or Iran might become so emboldened as to launch war directly with Israel, just to escalate this Holy War up to the next level—and try to bring back $100+ oil at the same time.

Anything that these players do at such a juncture would likely backfire on them...if not within a few months—then a few years. The rest of the world would quickly be up in arms against them, and we would all unite against their *"Axis of Evil Oil"—Mitch Reed, 2008*.

Then consider OPEC's own in fighting between all of the various players involved. These bastard countries will likely lead themselves towards their own self-interests, and their inability to hold the cartel together, and OPEC will eventually fade away and be no more...Allah Akbar!

And if, as I suspect that OPEC is in collusion with these Jihadist terrorists, as is Saudi Arabia at a minimum, think of the message we would send them!

How about we tell the Saudis:

"Naturally, as we end our relationship with your kingdom, this will include beginning an immediate and complete redeployment of our Saudi-based troops on an accelerated basis. We wish you lots of luck keeping your own fervently radical elements at bay without our military might to protect you...oh well, see ya fellas.

"Those elements who are forever threatening the overthrow of your House of Saud anyway (with Iranian help—no doubt) will likely finally get their chance—gosh, isn't that just a shame boys and girls? Hell, I guess if we're going to have to fight all these radical bastards anyway, we ought to let them take your vile and corrupt monarchy down first, and in so doing, help us to draw them out into the open, right here in Riyadh. Oh and by the way, your Royal pains in the pump—you're now on our lists of State Sponsors of Terrorism and the Axis of Evil Oil, at least for as long as you continue to exist, and did we mention we just froze all of your US-based assets too! Well, have a nice day guys."

Looking positively towards a greener future, whether climate change proves real by honest debate or not, we should learn to conserve and do a better job of protecting our planet, after all humans are responsible for the stewardship of this planet!

I hope that the implementation of this temporary rationing policy will also help to foster the right mindset among Americans to not only embrace some needed and desirable conservation, but hopefully giving public transportation and other alternatives a renewed focus as well.

We must get serious about weaning off of fossil fuels entirely within fifty or so years, that's a realistic target, despite what Al—*I'm green as anyone living in a mansion, flying on private jets and lounging on my cabin cruiser...can be Hypocritical*—Gore, believes. We need to look at specific bracketed goals by certain years and create the national mindset to reach them. This should be a no-fault, no blame, and bi-partisan policy of our country from this point forward.

Yet getting committed, means being realistic too. For one thing, we will have to monitor domestic conservation efforts through this fuel rationing closely to assure we can minimize tapping into our own Strategic Petroleum Reserve (SPR) in Alaska to no more than that initial contribution we discussed; there can be no daily shortfall therefore. Here's the deal, currently we have just short of seven hundred million barrels of crude oil in our SPR. This translates to a 58-day supply based on 12,040,000 barrels utilized per day as our net imports and we need to make that last a heck of a lot longer than 58 lousy days anyway, don't we? But here's the math on how I see this working with rationing. If we limit the tapping into our reserve to the one time three hundred million, we'll be sure to keep this vital asset, well—vital!

Look, we've covered 87% of the net daily imports of 12,040,000 barrels, that's 10,474,800 barrels, leaving a shortfall daily of 1,565,200 barrels a day of crude oil (13% shortfall) to eliminate by rationing hopefully. Assuming these numbers as a maximum—remain constant; this stretching of the number of days supply for our reserve will increase from 58 days to +/- 3,850 days...or over ten years of reserves available, based on the remaining near four hundred million barrels in the reserve divided by the roughly 1.5 million barrels a day shortfall. This is more than adequate to cover us while we increase our wells to new higher output locations, with more targeted exploration and drilling.

Of course, reducing our consumption through rationing to 1,565,200 fewer barrels will require an effort. Especially since there will need to be logical concessions built into the rationing policy.

Commercial trucking, including small business fleets for one thing, will need to be exempt and perhaps even given tax credits to help them stay in business and control their higher fuel expenses for diesel, in lieu of raising freight rates or product costs to their customers. This will depend naturally on how low gas and diesel falls.

But this one move alone, (tax credits) which could have been done when the crisis started months ago, will go a long way to helping minimize inflationary pressures within our trickle-down economy. Why isn't anyone in this Congress talking about this—from either party?

Commuters within smaller, rural communities with minimal public transportation and great expanses of distance between work and home destinations should also be exempt from rationing or given more flexibility. I.E. someone retired will be rationed, while a commuting worker will not, and will be given valuable concessions for embracing any fuel-saving alternatives available such as joining a carpool, etc.

On the other hand, residents of major cities with excellent public transportation should have slightly tighter rationing in place. Yet these cities should also be rewarded for their transportation infrastructure excellence, by receiving federal grants to improve their transportation systems further to zero emission, lower energy consumption, etc. Or help these cities provide municipal bond-based loans to their local cab companies to replace their Crown Victoria fleets with high MPG, low emission vehicles such as the awarding winning

Ford Fusion which is large enough for taxi use and will be available as a Hybrid this fall. The Fusion will mate a nearly 100 horsepower electric motor to an economical yet peppy multi-valve four cylinder motor with another 175 horsepower. City MPG may improve to as much as the 35 MPG milestone even in heavier urban traffic. With dramatic improvements like these, the local citizens win, our air quality and environment certainly win, our national MPG standards and conservation efforts win and American industry wins too.

Another winning concept is employers offering expansion of tele-commuting jobs, flex hours to minimize sitting in traffic, and/or free annual bus passes or van pools to their employees and then earning a dollar-for-dollar tax credit on their corporate income taxes from our Government? You see; we just have to think creatively.

Cities with lower excellence within their existing public transportation systems will need scrutiny and analysis. These cities' systems must be judged on their capacity and flexibility to expand their operations and routes quickly...and greenly. The federal government must support these local municipal efforts by offering tax incentives or other concessions, to enhance these systems where necessary, to greater serve their communities. You know, this has to be a national bi-partisan 'wake-up call' to work ideally.

One of the biggest pluses to what I am recommending here with rationing is the side effect of regaining a sane price for gas...and keeping it that way. Imagine, if gas goes back to $1.89 per gallon, the affect on our economy overall and every American's budget will get a shot in the arm and be more substantial than the recent stimulus passed by the Congress for a two-fold reason. The first is the obvious. Your gas purchases will be rationed to reduce the amount of gas you buy by 13 or so percent...I believe we should shoot for 15% minimum. Assuming you fill your 20 gallon tank once a week for all of your commuting needs and getting to work and back, that's like buying three (3) gallons less per week. At $1.89.9 per gallon, that's still a savings of $5.70 per week. But the second reason is naturally the more substantial one. By dropping the cost back to $1.89.9 per gallon in the first place, you'll save $2.17 per gallon, or a whopping $43.40 per 20 gallon tank, or a substantial...$188. per month over our current national average of $4.07 per gallon.

Naturally, there are nearly endless incentives available to use for this conservation policy change. Many are tried and true, some may be new and outside the box. The point is, our representatives in Congress must get busy, they must put their special interests aside...and they must go to work for a change!

One of the most beautiful things about Government incentives...is that they can be essentially painless for the Government in question to put out there. Let me give you an example of what I mean. One of the strongest incentives to any company or even say an individual who's an inventor is a tax 'credit'. The wonderful thing here is, is it's not the Government writing a single check to some company or person. It's nothing more than a minus sign on some line of the tax return that saves the company or individual some tax dollars, real savings to the company or person and yet almost painless participation by our lovely Government. So they get a few bucks less on April 15th...do you think it will greatly impact the government's revenues—hardly?

Another strong incentive from the Government would be something as simple as offering a 'Patent' incentive. Here's an example...and this costs the Government...not one penny: Our current basic patent laws for a utility patent grants I believe, twenty (20) years protection from competition on a patented invention, product, service, etc. All right, so here's a better idea. Why not offer the added incentive on all Petroleum-alternative or Petroleum-savings—awarded Patents that the number of years of protection increases to 50 years!

By increasing the covered years of protection from competition, you've given an individual firm or inventor—a tremendous intellectual property asset…and it has no inherent cost to the Government as all it amounts to is granting them additional years of no competition and therefore greater earnings and profits for an extended period of time…which translates to higher corporate income tax revenues, to the same Government, just to a different department, our friends at the IRS.

As a Government, we can also target our incentives and here again, with limited financial exposure. Here's yet another example and then I think the point's been made:

The United States is the equivalent of Saudi Arabia, when it comes to our current reserves of coal. In short, we have so much coal; we don't even know where to begin to utilize it. While coal is an abundant fossil fuel we possess, burning it comes into critical play because we must balance that desire, by the fact it is currently an inherently 'dirtier' fuel for our environment. All right, enough said.

What stops our Government from targeting this natural recourse then, that we have multitudes of decades of supply of, for more special incentives?

The government offers a challenge to industry to solve coal's shortcomings. By the way, other countries have already done this successfully! Allow both industry and individuals to participate in this competition. Set—a specific goal, or specific target. Then go further. Offer something else with this challenge…an added incentive. Create Century Royalty Patents. If successful, the winning entity enjoys up to one hundred (100) years of a preset modest royalty from any other company wishing to utilize their protected technology. Here in our example, it would be perfecting: Coal liquefaction: A successful chemical process, by which we can convert dirty coal into clean-burning liquid hydrocarbons, such as synthetic crude oil, and multiple ways to refine it into clean and plentiful gasoline and/or diesel.

Chapter Nine

My Playbook of Sorts vs. Theirs.

It goes without saying that I pray to God that our government will take heed of everything discussed so far, and the suggested steps I have already put forward in this last chapter, so that we may turn the corner on these powerful enemies and all of their allies.

We need to remove oil as a weapon in our enemy's arsenal that can be used against us. This is not a goal, it's a foregone necessity as already discussed. The only way to do this is to follow my suggestions at least on the outcome of no longer importing any oil from OPEC. A secondary plus is lessening Saudi Arabia's ability to transfer money to terrorists, and then ending this revenue stream permanently through the destruction of the Islamic Banking Industry, which certainly is complicit.

With this post-modern form of transnational warfare, we need to realize again, that our freedoms, liberties, and rights sometimes hurt more than help, in times of war like this.

Never doubt for a moment that strategists on their side like Naji, focus on using our legal system and our rights to *their* advantage, and that is perhaps the number one reason for their 'Infiltration Invasion' strategy with their parallel, yet shadowy communities.

As a pragmatic society, we must never forget our freedoms and rights are precious and paramount, but aren't we assuming that we are all playing by the same rules too? Our civil liberties must be protected for all of us to enjoy in a collective future. Without that collective future however, without our country, there will be no civil liberties worth saving!

So the collective future must at times, trump the civil liberties of individuals during times of great upheaval, such as war.

At all times, the greater good of the total society must always weigh heavier than the one individual. This is the core of the principle of eminent domain prevalent throughout common law practices of this and other countries.

This is why we have an executive branch of government, to exact the tough decisions. It is why FDR in example, felt compelled to intern Japanese Americans at the start of WWII to prevent hostilities and injuries between Americans.

What follows is our enemy's plan to infiltrate our society… *and clearly the two most important pages of this narrative.* A glimpse of the manifesto of Jihad against us from Plan 'B' awaits you.

We certainly must not allow any adversary to usurp our fundamental rights to on-going harmonious existence, in our collective future even in the name of something as precious as an individual's civil liberties…can we? Please keep these facts in mind as you read the following paragraphs, one day they may save your life:

"Naji's message is stark: Western civilization is doomed. Its last bastion, America, lacks the will for a long war. The 'infidel' loves life and treats it as an endless feast. <u>Jihadis have to ruin that feast</u> and persuade the 'infidel' to abandon this world in exchange for greater rewards in the next.

"Naji asks Jihadis to target oilfields, sea and airports, tourist facilities<u>, and especially banking and financial services.</u> He envisages "a very long war", at the end of which the whole world is brought under the banner of Islam.

"He identifies several Muslim countries as promising for establishing 'the governance of the wilderness': Saudi Arabia, Pakistan, Yemen, Turkey, Jordan, Libya, Tunisia and Morocco.

"The implication is that 'wilderness' units already exist in nations such as Afghanistan, Iraq, Lebanon, Egypt, Somalia and Algeria.

"Naji's theory is built on the concept of terror as the main organizing principle of the <u>mini-states</u> he hopes to set up everywhere in preparation for the coming Caliphate.

"In simple language, Naji offers a synthesis of the themes that appeal to different Jihadi groups. With anti-imperialist sentiments, missionary dreams, ethnic and class grievances, and puritanical obsessions, he mixes a deadly cocktail.

"No one should feel safe without submitting to Islam and those who refuse to submit…must pay a high price. The Islamist movement must aim to turn the world into a series of 'wildernesses' where only those under Jihadi rule enjoy security.

"Islamists in the 'wilderness' must create parallel societies alongside existing ones, Naji says- but do not set up formal governments, <u>which would be subject to economic pressure or military attack</u>.

"But they could also exist within cities, under the very noses of the authorities - <u>operating as secret societies with their own rules, values and enforcement</u>.

"But they could also take shape in <u>Western countries</u> with large Muslim minorities: The Jihadis are to begin by giving areas where Muslims live a distinctly Islamic appearance, by imposing special styles of dress for women and beards for men. Then they start imposing the shariah. In the final phase, they create a parallel system of taxation and law enforcement, effectively taking the areas out of government control"–Amir Taheri, July 2, 2008 New York Post.

Trust me, everything within these shadow communities will be centered on their Mosques or Madrassas and not even a 'fart' will go…unnoticed! To crack this bad egg open, someone's got to get inside and get the straight skinny, right from the source inside these secret societies.

I suggest we use the same exact strategies against our enemy that they plan on using on us! Since they want to infiltrate our communities with parallel shadow communities of their own, we should infiltrate their Mosques (and Madrassas if possible) from the start, with our own loyal group of operatives, Muslim or otherwise. Yet we don't stop there. Anywhere a new Mosque pops up, our forces must immediately begin a counter-shadow—shadow infiltration into the Jihadis' new parallel community. By opening shops and service businesses with operatives on staff that can eventually be drawn into their Mosques and their trust, we can stay one-step ahead of their plans.

So first and foremost…some long-term and invasive espionage is going to be in order here, courtesy of my first playbook idea…a new branch of the Armed Services; S.T.I.N.G.—Strategic-Tactics-In-National-Governance, the first Joint-Services, Antiterrorism Military Service Agency.

This new terror-fighting branch of service will be the first of its kind. Drawing jointly from the D.O.D. (tactically) and Homeland Security (politically) with tactical talent and strategy courtesy of all branches of the United States Military and our combined intelligence agencies, both military and domestic.

STING's head commander would report directly to a committee of the Joint Chiefs of Staff, the Secretary of Defense, and the Homeland Security Secretary. The designated liaison of this panel would report directly of course, to the Commander in Chief of the Armed Forces...AKA the President of the United States.

All four branches of service would offer their very best Special Forces and intelligence officers to initiate this fifth branch of service, by offering them the opportunity of exclusive assignment in this agency as STING-Elite-Rangers or STINGERs, concurrent to their present commissions.

Current special agents of the FBI and CIA would also be eligible to enlist in STING as well. These agents of the Intelligence services would have the honor to enlist at the rank of Captain, given their officers school equivalency, offered by the Intelligence Agency academies they graduated from.

STINGERs will specialize in and bring Antiterrorism theory and action into a central powerhouse and legitimate branch of the Armed Services as its sole, yet comprehensive domain. At once, we will have a focused access and coordinated effort to all of the very best elite service personnel and training techniques.

STING will be focused on preventing, tracking, and countermanding all terrorism concerns and activities. In all matters of terrorism, STING will oversee and coordinate all non-STING military mobilizations and strategies, and all first-responder coordination, along with border security responsibility. Finally, we give our borders the comprehensive protection they need, under US Military security, and consequently, our borders will finally be closed and secured!

Under one roof, we assemble experts on surveillance, intelligence, counter-intelligence, high technology, theological history, profiling, weapons, biologics and WMD, cyber tactics and supremacy, explosives, special ops, infiltration, financial warfare, & linguistics, etc.

We combine everything we've learned from our most elite Special Forces and intelligence units, along with what our enemies have taught us, and meld them into a centralized and focused branch of service, doing one thing only and doing it better than anyone, a terrorism taskforce if you will! Now let's move on.

Here's a little legal conundrum to test your knowledge on terrorist organizations. Why not knock on the door of the Islamic Thinkers Society in New York City without a search warrant, and see how long it takes them to point that fact out to you!

Likely, they will make one telephone call to their best friend, their legal mentors, their saviors, the A.C.L.U. Please don't get me started on these clowns, believe me. Just read O'Reilly's Culture Warrior and double it, and you'd be getting close to my feelings on the subject of the A.C.L.U.

My second playbook suggestion therefore, is forming a blue ribbon panel of constitutional scholars, and charge them with the task of researching precedent, torte law, our US codes and laws, Executive Order options, etc. and to come up with some definitive ways to curb the inherent excesses within our 'freedoms'…for the people who are truly in our communities strictly as future or current enemy combatants. Currently, these enemies of our country, enjoy too free of a society, and that includes disarming any ancillary or nuisance organizations as well that enable them such as the A.C.L.U.

To begin with, legislate or order limits of any organization's involvement with an enemy combatant during a time of conflict or wartime. Further, limit these organizations to representing only the rights of American Citizens and/or documented residents, on strictly non-wartime-related matters, and under no circumstances whatsoever, for undocumented individuals, or suspected enemy combatants. All such cases should be brought before the war tribunal system. When the ACLU balks at this, it will be necessary to slow them down and put them in their place, one way, or the other.

Have this blue ribbon panel present their recommendations to the Attorney General, complete with referenced precedents, etc. to develop an expanded version of the current Patriot Act, this time focused on the latest specific threats from Al Qaeda's Plan B and their Infiltration Invader approach.

Despite what the Supreme Court recently did in their Habeas Corpus ruling this July, we must keep these radicals clearly within the classification of enemy combatants and not subject to our Criminal Justice System—but rather the Military Tribunals afforded to all war criminals. Even if they are Infiltration Invaders or Cells, living in the US legitimately, this is an absolute necessity. If necessary, President Bush should invoke his privilege to demand this by Executive Order. Remember, our enemy will do everything possible to legitimize any of their operatives and use our legal system against us wherever possible, as we get wise to their plans.

And I must briefly mention as well that: So far…shame on 'W' and of course Congress, for not calling the Supreme Court on the carpet for their Habeas Corpus decision and not already countermanding it.   Lincoln would have, and where's FDR when we need him? He too clearly understood the limitations of the courts under the Separation of Powers, and the power of the Executive Order. He honestly needs to be miraculously brought back from the grave so that he can train 'W' and his successor on how to overcome this in the future. Whatever it takes to keep our country safe and sound during wartime! *"Franklin Roosevelt was president for a little over twelve years. In that time, he issued 3,723 executive orders, a figure greater than the total issued by all succeeding presidents through the end of the Clinton administration."—Excerpt from the book: Inside the Shadow Government National Emergencies and the Cult of*

Secrecy—By Harry Helms, Feral House, 2003, paper. As posted on the Third World Traveler on the Internet

Remember under our three branches of government, the Judiciary branch at the Supreme Court is charged with upholding the US Constitution, and not over-stepping into the other branches' areas. Clearly the Supreme Court did this to many observers point of view, with their recent Habeas Corpus decision.

My third playbook idea is to establish an Americans' Wartime Responsibilities Order as an expansion of the Patriot Act, perhaps titled the American Patriots Proclamation. I would prefer that both be made law by Executive Order of President Bush…there will be less gray area that way, in my opinion…and he's got the cojonies to do it besides! In these orders, I would like to see him suggest suitable and fair behaviors, for all Americans to hopefully embrace and abide by, during this long war we will have to wage, until we hopefully achieve our victory.

Naturally, there should be numerous safeguards contained to assure the rights of Americans are held at the highest level of preciousness, while still protecting our Country's vital safety and interests…our collective future.

All Americans share responsibilities to their country during this and any war, and I believe it is only fair that the country and our leaders spell those responsibilities out, so everyone follows the same drummer for once, united and committed to our common good and mutual survival!

To my friends on the right or left who vehemently oppose any Presidential Executive Order simply on principle…and declare it illegal, unconstitutional, or whatever, remember that presidents have used executive orders extensively and they invariably seem to mostly hold up in the courts and with Congress. President Lincoln used this power to free the slaves. The Emancipation Proclamation was after all, an Executive

Order.—*Harry Helms, Feral House, 2003, paper. As posted on the Third World Traveler on the Internet*

I welcome any debate from my friends on either side concerning this suggestion, but once it's passed, I would hope that they along with all Americans, honor our country first, by embracing it.

A Brief Summation

Perhaps it's ironic, yet still satisfying to mention that as I initially write this summation, the date just changed to July 4th, 2008.

This should be a day of family, fireworks, celebration, and harmony, rather than having to fight a war.

Still, half way around the world, our brave heroes are at war, a war that sadly seems to be in its opening chapters. Perhaps if we could all come together and focus our efforts— we could change that prognosis!

Thanks to a brilliant, candid, and poignant film, you likely realize what we will be up against in the ensuing years without some form of reenergized intervention, or change of heart by our enemies and that's not likely.

To those reading this who are religious and witnesses to a well-worn and read bible…whatever version, might I indulge you to pray for our Country and our people. It wouldn't hurt for more of us to do that either, believe me. For those who fear or would suggest that this conflict may lead to or be our Armageddon or Revelations, again I certainly indulge your prayers.

We are not simply Democrats, Republicans, Libertarians, and Independents—we are first and foremost Americans. We are no longer fighting for our individual politics and beliefs—we will be fighting for the right to live and to enjoy a collective future together, so that we may be able to go on disagreeing for yet another day.

So, we are in the beginning moments, of perhaps a long, horrific, and brutal war for our very survival as men and women in a free country of free thinkers, possessing great freedoms and rights.

Fellow Americans…friends, it's time we ask ourselves the same question that's been put forth to every generation of free men and women that have come before us at one time or another: Who seeks my destruction, let me look upon his face once…before I vanquish him?

So there you have it, and the cat's out of the bag now and has all nine lives left to torment us, so all bets are off the table. The question becomes—what are you going to do about it?

Thank you for your read.

Please visit my blog: Reeditandweep.com or my book site for information on my published books and works in progress: BooksbyMitchReed.com.

You can email me at: MitchReed@hotmail.com, but please put "Book" in your subject line, if you expect me to receive your mail.

Please visit www.Obsessionthemovie.com to order your copy of Obsession.

THINK ABOUT IT!

"In time, this so-called democracy will crumble, and there will be nothing, and the only thing that will remain will be Islam." Imam Siraj Wahhaj.—Fox News Online, July 21, 2008